MAGIC YOUR MIND HAPPY

AMAZING magic tricks for HAPPINESS, CONFIDENCE and CALM

The author is not responsible for any adverse effects resulting from the use of the information presented in this book and this information is not intended to be a substitute for consulting with a healthcare or education professional.

First published in Great Britain in 2024 by Wren & Rook

Text copyright © SPIN SOLUTIONS LIMITED 2024
Illustrations copyright © Luke Newell 2024
All rights reserved.

The right of Richard Wiseman and Luke Newell to be identified as the author and illustrator respectively of this Work has been asserted by them in accordance with the Copyright, Designs & Patents Act 1988.

ISBN: 978 1 5263 6650 4

1 3 5 7 9 10 8 6 4 2

Wren & Rook
An imprint of
Hachette Children's Group
Part of Hodder & Stoughton
Carmelite House
50 Victoria Embankment
London EC4Y 0DZ

An Hachette UK Company
www.hachette.co.uk
www.hachettechildrens.co.uk

Printed and bound in Great Britain by Clays Ltd, Elcograf S.p.A.

Contents

Welcome to the Show
9

Your Magic Toolkit
16

Superpower 1
Increase Your Confidence by Magic
19

Superpower 2
Achieve the Impossible with Some Incredible Illusions
43

Superpower 3
Make Friendships Appear
61

Superpower 4
Master Magical Teamwork
81

Superpower 5
Ace Resilience
99

Superpower 6
Grow Your Curiosity
115

Superpower 7
Improve Focus and Boost Your Brain Power
137

Superpower 8
Conjure up Creativity
157

Finale
183

About the Author
191

WELCOME TO THE SHOW

Welcome! My name is Richard Wiseman, and I'm a psychologist, which means that I like to explore how minds work. I'm also a real-life magician, which means that I love to perform magic tricks.

Let me start by saying:

THANK YOU FOR READING THIS AND LET'S GET ON WITH THE THE SHOW.

Wait a minute, did you notice that the sentence on the previous page said: 'the the show'? If you did spot the word 'the' written twice, then congratulations! And if, like most readers, you missed them, then I hope that this little illusion made you **smile**. This book is going to be full of **surprising tricks** that you can use to amuse yourself, and to amaze your friends and family.

However, unlike other books on magic tricks, I hope that this one will bring some REAL MAGIC into your life. But more about that later.

Let me tell you something about myself. I am fascinated by magic and saw my first magic trick when I was seven years old, while visiting my grandfather. He was slow on his feet, forgot stuff and couldn't hear very well. However, like everyone, there were many things about him that were wonderful. He was kind, thoughtful and loving. Best of all, he could perform an **AMAZING** magic trick!

It began with him handing me a marker pen and a coin, and asking me to write my initials on the coin. Then, he carefully placed the coin in the palm of his hand and gently closed his fingers around it. When he opened his hand, **the coin had disappeared**. My mouth dropped open in amazement!

WHAT!?!? HOW DID THAT HAPPEN?

But there was more to come. My grandfather reached under his chair and took out a small metal tin that was sealed with several elastic bands. He asked me to remove the bands and to open the tin. Inside, I discovered a small wooden box that was sealed with more elastic bands. When I opened the wooden box . . . I found my initialled coin inside.

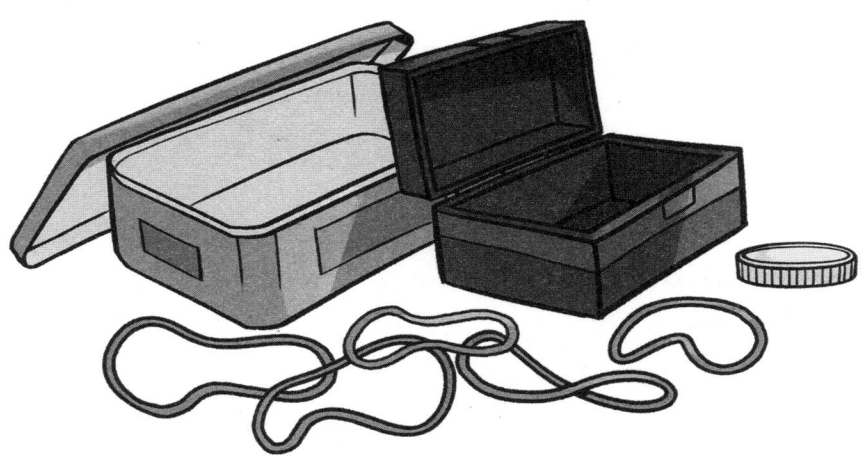

IMPOSSIBLE!!!! ARRGGHHHHHH!!!!!!

I could never work out how my grandfather performed his illusion. Then, one day, he told me that the secret was written in a mysterious book, hidden in the local library. I went along to the library and read *all* the magic books. Eventually, I came across the secret to my grandfather's remarkable trick.

Those books introduced me to the fascinating, strange and secretive world of magic. I discovered how magicians **pluck coins from behind people's ears**, **saw people in half** (and, on a good night, put them back together again!) and **levitate high into the air**. I spent lots of time rehearsing my favourite tricks, and I eventually performed at parties and in theatres. When I was twenty-two, I even travelled to the USA to perform my magic act in Hollywood (although the trip turned out to be a disaster – more about that later!).

I quickly discovered that good magicians understand how their audiences see the the world. For instance, an illusionist needs to make you look in one place while they do something somewhere else. They also must know how to make you miss the two 'the's in the sentence above (again, well done if you spotted them).

Because of the close relationship between **magic and the mind**, I became a **psychologist** and spent lots of time studying how we think, feel and behave. A few years ago, I discovered something remarkable.

Most people want to know how magicians perform their amazing illusions. However, master illusionists have carefully guarded these secrets for thousands of years (except when one of them accidentally left a safe door open, and the entire

world discovered how to change a tea towel into a chicken!). But here's their **biggest and best-kept secret:**

LEARNING MAGIC GIVES YOU AMAZING POWERS! IT CAN HELP YOU TO BECOME EVEN MORE CONFIDENT, POPULAR, SMART AND CREATIVE.

And that's what this book is all about.

I AM GOING TO TEACH YOU HOW TO PERFORM JAW-DROPPING, MIND-BLOWING MAGIC TRICKS!

You will discover how to **defy gravity, read minds, produce coins from behind your friend's ear, predict the future** and much more. I will even show you my all-time favourite trick — **how to change a tea towel into a chicken!** But most important of all, during our time together I hope that you will also gain **eight superpowers — important life skills that will make you even more wonderful.**

GADGETS BE GONE!

Before we begin, let's make your smartphones, tablets and computers disappear by putting them out of reach. Rather than staring at a screen, this book encourages you to use your hands to create magical apparatus and make ordinary objects do extraordinary things. And once you have learned a few tricks, you can use them to have fun, connect with people face to face (or IRL!) and make your friends and family say . . .

HA!!! WOW!!! NO WAY!!!!

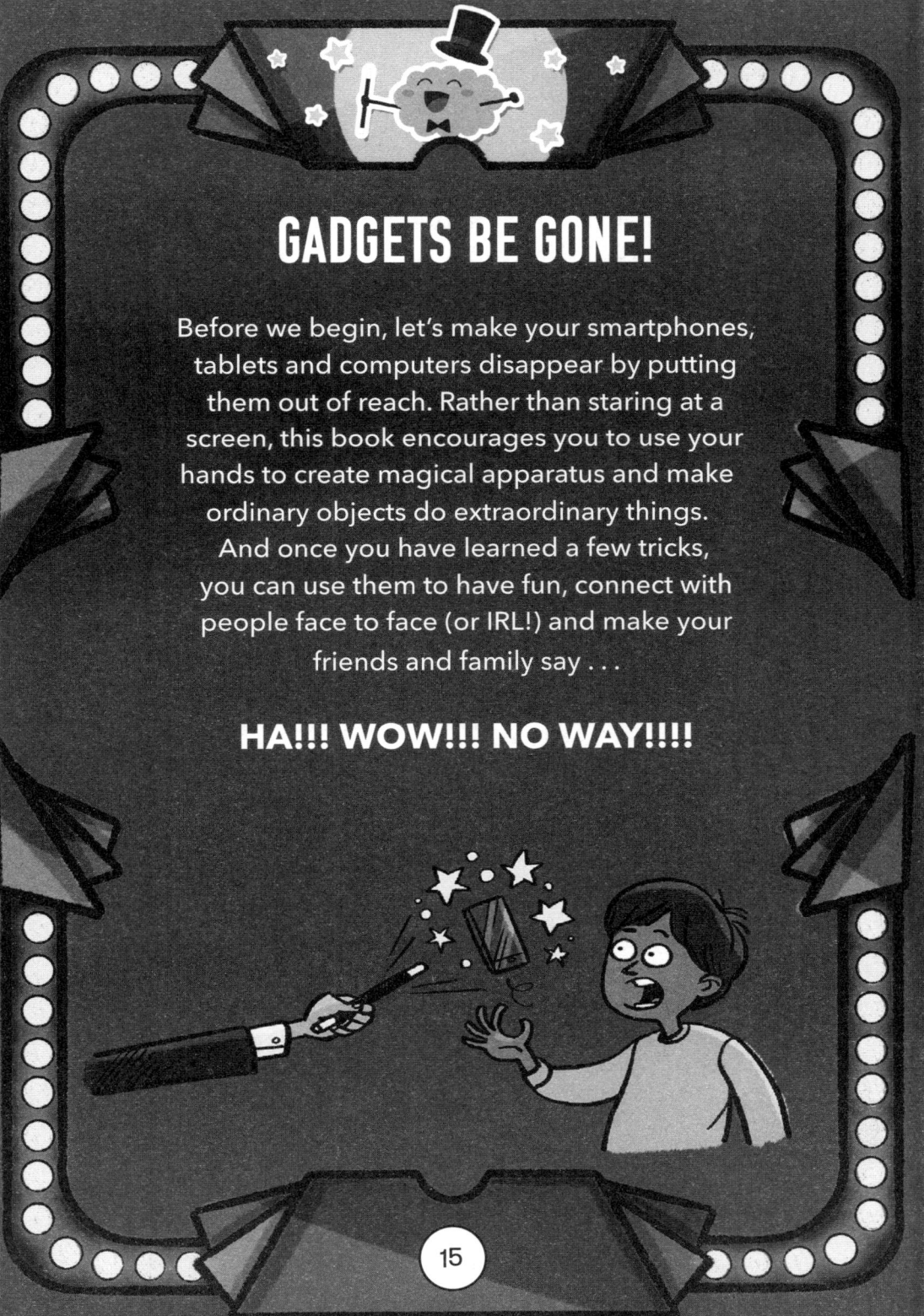

You can probably find all the objects that you will need around your home. Together they will form:

YOUR MAGIC TOOLKIT

Here's a selection of things to gather up so they're ready for when you start trying out the magic tricks.

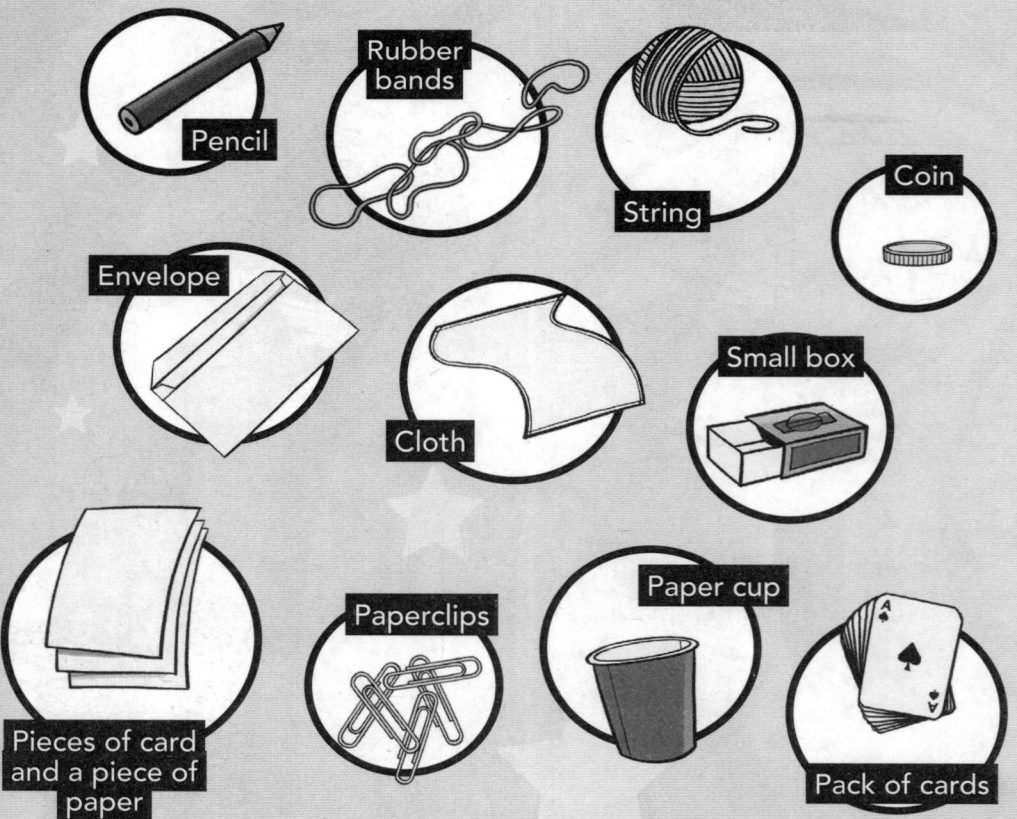

It's time to introduce the star of the show. They are astonishing, amazing and brilliant . . .

DRUM ROLL

. . . It's . . .

YOU!

SUPERPOWER 1

INCREASE YOUR CONFIDENCE BY MAGIC

I love performing magic tricks in front of large groups of people, but I haven't always been like that. When I was a child, I wasn't very confident, but magic helped me because it involved learning difficult tricks and doing things that other people couldn't do. Magic gave me a boost and that made me want to get even better at it, because the more I did it, the more confident I became!

Are you ready to try a few magic tricks?

Right now, you might be thinking something like . . .

I WON'T BE VERY GOOD AT THIS!

. . . or maybe . . .

BUT WHAT IF I MESS UP?

These types of thoughts can pop up in your mind when you don't feel very confident. Let's make them **disappear** with the help of some quick and easy illusions, starting with . . .

THE FLOATING SAUSAGE!

Let me introduce you to your hands. (Hello, hands!) On each hand you have a thumb, a first finger, a second finger, a third finger and a little finger.

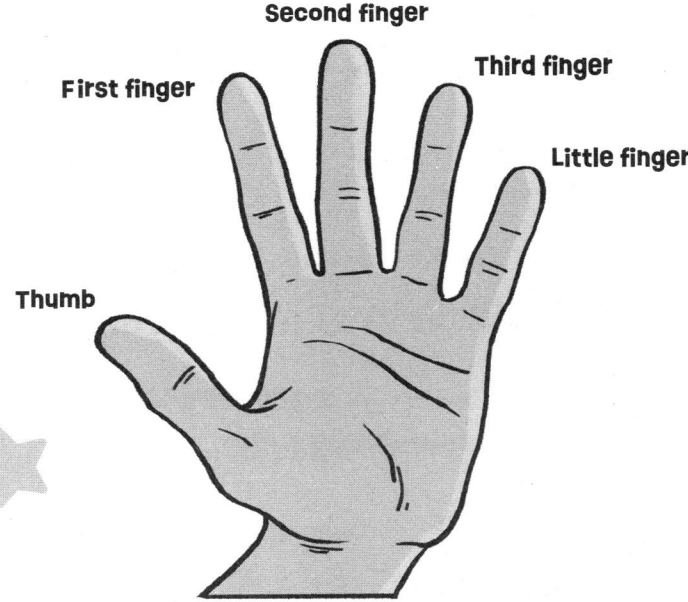

We are going to use your hands to make a sausage float in front of your eyes!

> **This fun illusion was discovered in 1928 by a psychologist called Winford Lee Sharp.**

Extend both first (pointing) fingers and place the tips together like this.

Hold them about 30 cm in front of your nose and focus on an object on the other side of the room.

Relax your eyes. All being well, **a tiny sausage will appear between your fingertips!**

When that happens, move your hands a few millimetres apart and you will see **a floating sausage!**

Now you know how it feels to see something surprising, delightful and magical. Not only that, but you have performed your first illusion. Congratulations!

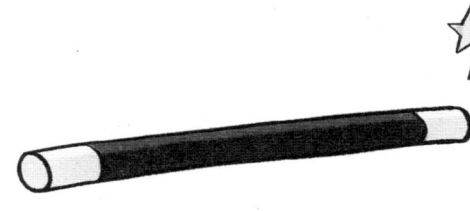

Let's try another quick trick.

MIND CONTROL!

Place one hand, palm down, on a table and then carefully bend your second finger underneath so that the middle joint rests on the table. Like this:

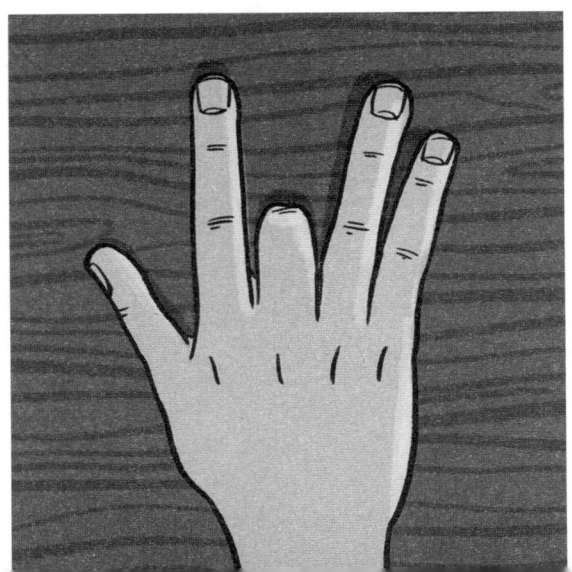

The tip of your second finger should be close to your palm.

Next, move your first finger up and down, so that you are tapping it on the table.

Do the same thing with your little finger.

SO FAR, SO WHAT?

Now I am going to use my mind power to stop you moving your third finger!

Try to move your third finger up and down. You will probably find it very difficult, and most people can't move their finger at all. Some people are very flexible and can move their third finger – if that's you, congratulations!

As you might have guessed, this illusion has **nothing to do with mind power**. Moving your fingers involves thick bands of tissue called tendons. Your first finger and little finger each have their own tendon. However, your third finger shares a tendon with your second finger. When you bend your second finger under your hand, you put that tendon out of action and so you will probably struggle to move your third finger.

Now you can perform two illusions and, hopefully, you will be feeling **more confident** about learning **magic tricks**.

Let's move to the next level and try a trick with **an object!**

THE BENDY PENCIL

This fun illusion can be performed with any long, straight object, like a pencil, a pen or a straw. Let's try it with a pencil.

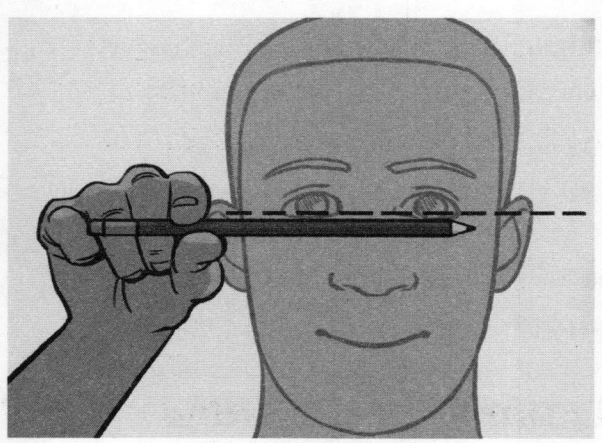

Hold the pencil between your thumb and first finger, about a quarter of the way from one end. Make sure that the pencil is horizontal and at eye level.

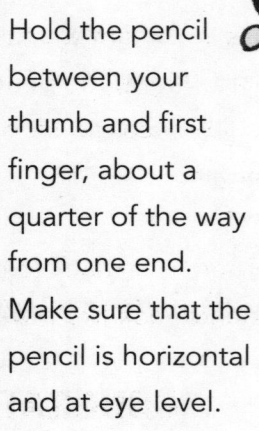

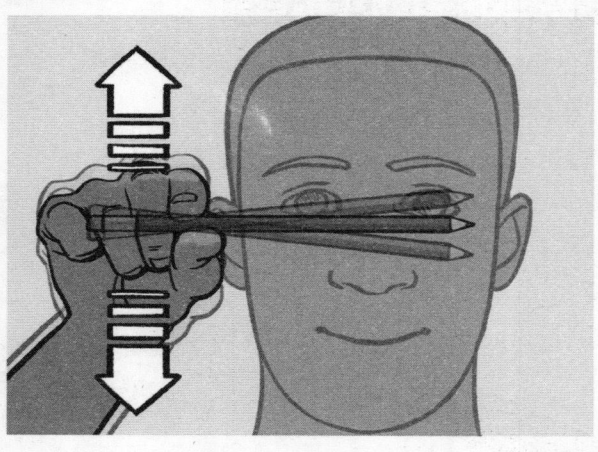

Now jiggle the pencil up and down several times. Each time, move your hand about 2 cm up and then about 2 cm down.

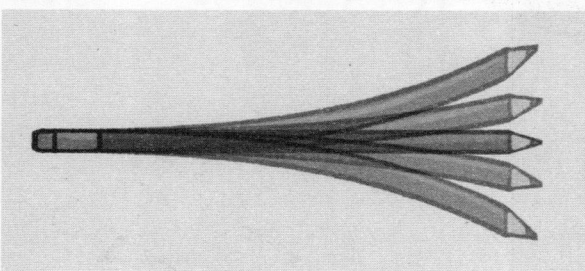

Now keep moving the pencil up and down but loosen your grip on it, so that it wiggles between your thumb and finger.

It's important to make the movements nice and smooth. If you get it right, the pencil will appear to be bendy and soft. After a few seconds, stop wiggling the pencil and it will look solid again.

There is a knack to it, so keep trying until you can make the pencil look like it was made from rubber!

CONGRATULATIONS, YOU CAN NOW PERFORM THREE ILLUSIONS!

I became fascinated by magic when I was about eight years old. After learning a few tricks, I rushed to school and showed them to all my classmates. However, sometimes I made mistakes because I hadn't practised them properly. Although most of my friends were encouraging, a few of them said things like . . .

I CAN SEE HOW IT'S DONE

YOU'RE NOT VERY GOOD

IT'S UP YOUR SLEEVE

Maybe they didn't like being fooled, or wanted to make me feel bad, or were being honest. It wasn't great for my confidence.

So, how do we **get confident** at performing magic tricks? Here are my top tips:

Start by practising the first three tricks in this book **on your own**.

Once you're ready to show your magic skills to others, **pick a few supportive friends** or family members and explain to them that you are trying to learn some magic, and ask them if they would mind watching you perform a trick. That way, their expectations will be lower, and they will understand that they are helping you to **practise and to become more confident**.

If you feel nervous about performing tricks in front of an audience, **try taking one or two deep breaths to calm yourself**. Also, try telling yourself that your **nerves are a sign of being excited**. It's fine if something goes wrong, because you can all just laugh together about it.

After you have performed your tricks, it's a good idea to **ask your audience for feedback**. Listen to what they say and see if it can help you to improve.

5 Get a notebook and jot down the tricks that you performed and how they went, along with the feedback so you can use it to improve.

> **REMEMBER:**
>
> **These tips don't just apply to learning magic tricks – in everyday life you can become more confident by practising, learning from your mistakes, taking on feedback and trying again.**

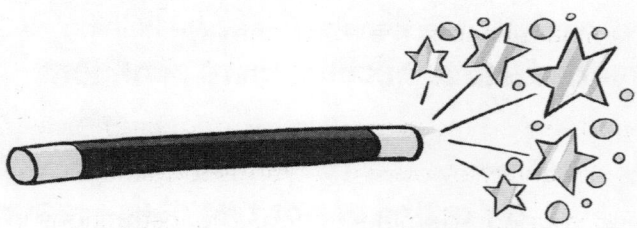

Now let's move on to a trick that requires more time and patience. This will be challenging but it will be worth it because it will make people say . . .

WOW, NO WAY!

THE AMAZING JUMPING BAND

This wonderful trick involves making a rubber band magically jump between your fingers. It was invented more than a hundred years ago by a clever British magician called Stanley Collins.

You will need a rubber band or a hair tie that fits over your first and second fingers.

Let me tell you more about your hands. Almost everyone has a **dominant** and a **non-dominant** hand. Your dominant hand is the one that you usually write with and your non-dominant hand is the other one.

Most people find it easier to do secret magic moves with their dominant hand. However, if you are struggling to learn a trick, try using your non-dominant hand. The instructions in this book are written as if your dominant hand is your right hand. If you are left-handed, then reverse the instructions.

Before you perform the trick, you need to get your right hand and the band in the correct position. Put the band over the first and second fingers of your right hand and move it all the way down.

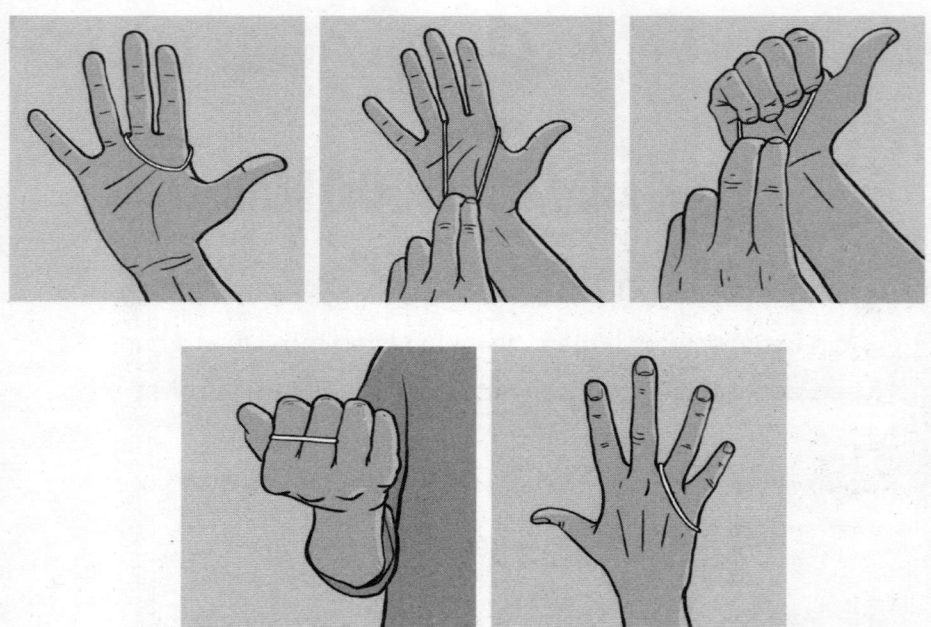

With your left hand, carefully stretch the band towards yourself.

Bend all four fingers of your right hand inside the loop of the band and then release the band so that it lies across your fingernails. Now you are ready to perform the trick.

Show your friend the back of your right hand. To them, it will look like the band is wrapped around your first and second fingers.

Now say the word 'jump'. Keeping all your fingers together, quickly open your right hand, pushing the band up with all four fingers. The band will magically jump from your first and second fingers to your third and little fingers.

KEEP PRACTISING!

To perform the amazing jumping-band trick well, you need to be able to carry out the hand movements smoothly. There is only one way of achieving this – practise! Place a rubber band in your pocket or in a bag, and keep taking it out, putting it on your fingers and carrying out the secret move until you can complete the trick in one smooth movement.

It's sometimes helpful to see how the trick looks from your friend's perspective by looking in a mirror.

As you practise, you will make mistakes. I did that too. Sometimes I put the band on the wrong fingers, or I didn't carry out the secret move smoothly. Then there were the times when I opened my hand too quickly and the band flew across the room, and once I was so surprised by the illusion that my ears fell off (I made that last one up).

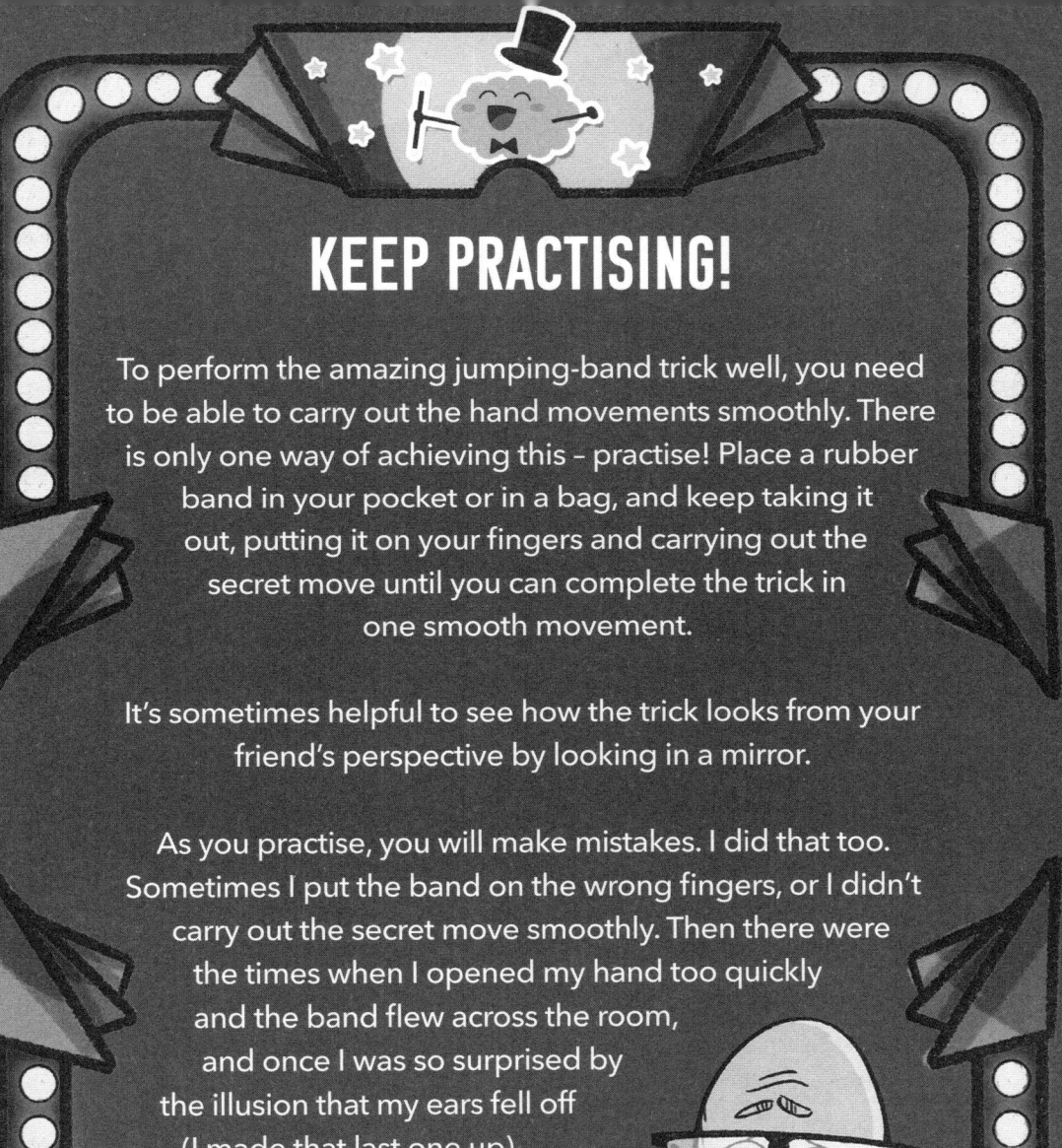

When you make mistakes, you might find yourself thinking something like . . .

I AM NOT GETTING ANY BETTER

I BET OTHER PEOPLE ARE BETTER THAN ME

I CAN'T DO THIS

Instead of being put off when you make mistakes, see them as helpful signposts that show you where you need to improve. There's an old saying that goes: people who make no ~~misttakes~~ ~~missstakes~~ ~~mmistakes~~ mistakes make nothing! If you are worried that you are not improving, **be kind to yourself**. Also, **think about what a good friend would say to you**. Here are **my top tips for being kind to yourself:**

★1 Think about what you are doing well. Remember that even a small amount of progress is still progress!

★2 Try not to worry about what other people can and can't do. It's **you** that matters. If you do want to compare yourself to others, use them as a source of **inspiration**. No one was born being able to make a band jump between their fingers. Instead, they learned how to do it – and so can you.

★3 Remember the magic word! So, what's the magic word? Abracadabra? No! Please? Sometimes . . . but on this occasion, it's **'yet'**. This little word is small but mighty because it can change how you think when faced with big challenges. It's something that can **grow your self-belief and confidence** – even top athletes use it to achieve their goals!

Here's how it works: when you think, 'I can't do this,' add the magic word 'yet' to the end of the sentence so that it becomes:

I can't do this... yet!

This is more positive because it suggests that you will be able to do it in the future. Also, think about the amazing things that

you couldn't do in the past but can do now. Maybe you can ride a bike, or say a few words in French, or make a cheese sandwich. You learned how to do these things and you can master this new trick too.

> **The idea of using the magic word 'yet' originally came from the psychologist Carol Dweck.**

Once you have mastered the jumping-band trick, you will need to practise saying something while you perform the illusion. Maybe try something like . . .

This band is amazing. (Place the band over your two fingers.)

It doesn't move through my fingers. (Stretch the band and carry out the secret move.)

But when I say JUMP, it suddenly jumps to my other two fingers! (Open your fingers and the band will jump across.)

Congratulations on learning a much harder piece of magic, and some brilliant life skills too.

HOSPITAL MAGIC

Magic is used in hospitals to help patients get better. Learning magic makes patients feel happier because it boosts their confidence, creates a sense of achievement and gives them something fun to show their visitors and the people looking after them.

Some time ago, American magician David Copperfield set up a pioneering initiative called Project Magic. This wonderful scheme encourages magicians, doctors and nurses to help patients learn to perform magic tricks. Lots of other groups have carried out similar work across the world. For example, in the Netherlands, an organisation called Magic Care arranges for magicians to go into hospitals to teach magic to children.

In the UK, the Breathe Magic Intensive Therapy Programme uses magic to help young people who have a weakness, or paralysis, that affects one side of their body. Scientists have discovered that the tricks improve movements and dexterity because they are a fun way of encouraging people to repeat important actions again and again.

Now you can play with different versions of the amazing rubber-band trick because your magic is like you – it **develops and grows** over time. Let's explore fun ways of presenting this trick.

- You could say that the band is a great athlete and will attempt the long jump, or that it is made from a new kind of hi-tech rubber, or that you can perform the fastest magic trick in the world! Try different presentations and see which one feels best for you.

- After you are ready to make the band jump, try holding your fist sideways. Then move your hand up and down as you quickly open and close it. The big up-and-down movement helps to hide the opening and closing of your hand.

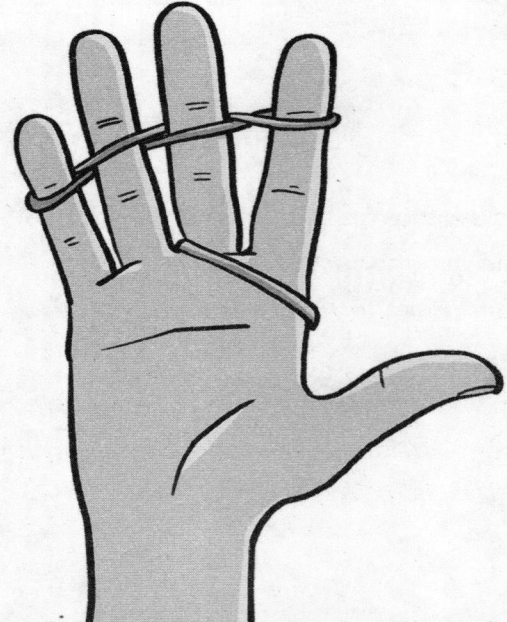

- Try twisting a second band across the top of your fingers. Amazingly, the first band will still jump between your fingers! (This is great to do after you have shown someone the basic version.) A magician named Theo Bamberg came up with this idea about ten years after the illusion was invented. Magic is like everyday life. **Good things take time to develop and grow.**

Again, perform these different versions of the illusion to supportive friends and family members, and see what they think. You will soon find that people are either fooled or they are not.

That's another reason why magic is great – it gives you a clear goal to aim for because people must be amazed each time you perform a trick.

When you feel confident and comfortable, try showing the different versions of the trick to other people too.

At the start of this chapter, you may not have felt confident about being a magician. But now, you can perform some jaw-dropping feats and do lots of things that other people can't do!

We began with some simple illusions to **build up your confidence**. Once you could perform those, we moved on to a more difficult trick. After you mastered that, we added some moves that were **even more challenging**. Along the way, we discovered **how to deal with negative thoughts** and celebrated each time you mastered the next stage.

You can use the same ideas in everyday life. For example, maybe you want to do even better at school, learn a new skateboard move, create some wonderful art or become an astronaut?

WHATEVER YOU WANT TO DO:

MAKE A START,
TAKE IT ONE STEP AT A TIME,
LEARN FROM YOUR MISTAKES,
AND PAT YOURSELF ON THE BACK
WHENEVER YOU MAKE SOME
PROGRESS!

TOGETHER, THESE MAGICAL
IDEAS WILL HELP YOU TO FEEL
FAR MORE CONFIDENT!

SUPERPOWER 2

ACHIEVE THE IMPOSSIBLE WITH SOME INCREDIBLE ILLUSIONS

Magicians do extraordinary things all the time, and in this chapter, I will teach you how to think like a magician and make the seemingly impossible possible!

Let's begin with one of my favourite puzzles.

THE TIE-A-KNOT PUZZLE

Find a piece of string that is about 60 cm long.* Hold one end in your left hand and the other end in your right hand. Can you tie a knot in the string without letting go of the ends?

How did you get on? Most people quickly give up because it seems **impossible**. But not magicians! They make extraordinary things happen all the time, and they think about new and unusual ways forward. They try and fail. Then try again and fail again. Then they try some more and – BINGO! – they come up with a wonderful idea that makes everyone say . . .

ARRRGGHHH. WHY DIDN'T I THINK OF THAT!!!

*You can also use a long rolled-up napkin or cloth, a scarf or a tie.

Have you figured out a solution to the tie-a-knot challenge? While you are thinking about it, let's talk about **assumptions**. These are ideas and thoughts that we take for granted. For instance, we might see the front of a blue jumper and assume that the back is blue too. Or we might see three legs of a chair and assume that there is a fourth leg.

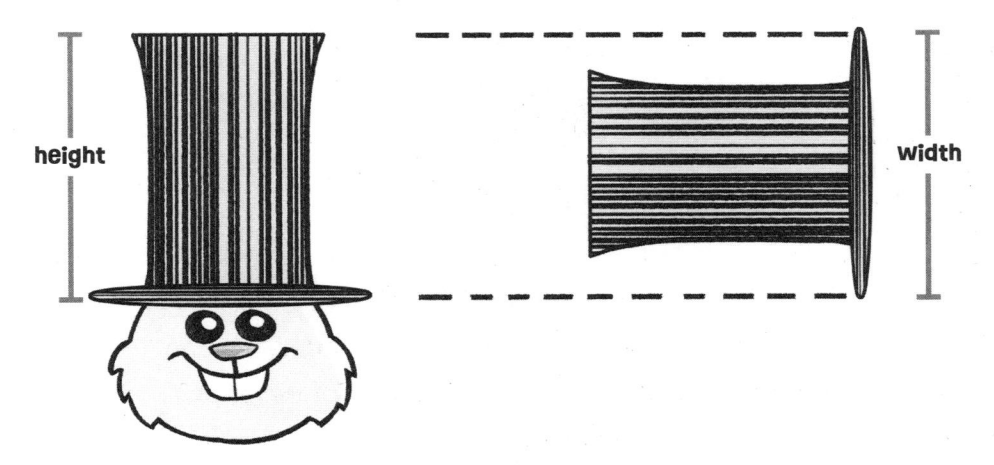

height

width

Or we might glance at this picture of a top hat and assume that the height of the hat is bigger than the width of the brim. Most of the time these assumptions are correct, but sometimes they are wrong. For instance, if you measure the top hat in the picture, you will discover that the height of the hat is the same as the width of the brim!

Our incorrect assumptions sometimes stop us seeing solutions that are right in front of our eyes. During the tie-a-knot puzzle, you probably assumed that your arms should start uncrossed.

Most people do. But what happens when we question this assumption?

Try the puzzle again, but this time . . .

Place the string on a table and cross your arms.

Now lean to the right and pick up one end of the string in your left hand.

Next, lean to the left and pick up the other end of the string in you right hand.

Finally, carefully unfold your arms, making sure that you do not let go of the ends. A knot will appear on the string. We thought like a magician and found a simple and smart way of making **the seemingly impossible possible!**

There are lots of things you can do to help you come up with new and unusual ways of making extraordinary things happen. Here are three of my favourite techniques:

1 EXPLORE

Discover how other people have solved similar problems. Read books, search the internet (with permission from your grown-up!) and chat to your friends and family. How can other people's ideas help you? What is everyone assuming? What happens when you do the opposite to everyone else?

2 KEEP GOING

It's often tempting to go with the first solution that comes into your mind. Resist the temptation! Try to think of more ideas and answers, and don't worry if they are silly or impractical. Then look at all your solutions and choose the best one.

3 RELAX

Take a break. Maybe go for a walk, kick a ball around, work on another problem or sleep on it and see if you wake up with an idea. Maybe keep a notebook by your bed so that you can write down your ideas before they vanish from your mind. It's surprising how often a wonderful solution will suddenly pop into your head when you are doing something else.

Let's see if these techniques can help us solve some other seemingly impossible puzzles.

Imagine that you are a driving a bus to a magic show and have three magicians on board. At the next bus stop, one magician gets off and another two magicians board the bus. Then, at the following stop, four more magicians climb aboard and three magicians leave. At the final stop, one magician gets off and two more magicians get on.

The question is . . . **what's the bus driver's name?**

Most people carefully count the passengers getting on and off the bus and think that it's impossible to know the driver's name. But let's do the opposite to them and see what happens. Instead of focusing on the passengers, look somewhere else. Have you spotted the solution yet? If not, read the first sentence of the puzzle. It says that you are the driver and so the answer is . . . your name!

HOW TO PUT YOUR HEAD THROUGH A POSTCARD

For the next puzzle you will need a postcard or a similar-sized piece of thin cardboard. Can you make a hole in the postcard and put your head through it? Again, it seems impossible, and most people quickly give up. But let's think like a magician, believe that it's possible and see if we can come up with a clever solution.

Well . . . you could carefully make a hole in the postcard, take a photograph of your head and slide it through. **We did it!**

It would be easy to give up now, because we have an answer. However, there might be an even better solution, so let's think of some other ideas. Maybe it will help to go for a walk or play outside.

Hold on, here's another idea. You could write the words 'YOUR HEAD' on a piece of paper and put that through the hole.

And here's another thought. You could use some yet-to-be-invented technology to make yourself tiny. That's interesting, but not very practical.

How about somehow making the postcard huge? Again, not very practical. But what if you made the card into an object that you could put over your head? You can put a necklace over your head. Could you convert the postcard into a necklace? There's lots of clever paper folding and origami out there, so maybe you could find out if that would help?

Try this for size.

Fold the postcard in half lengthways and use a pair of scissors to carefully cut along the vertical lines marked below.* Make sure that you cut the card on both sides of the fold.

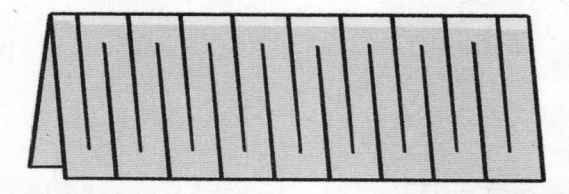

Remember, safety first! Be careful when you are using scissors and always ask an adult to help you.

Next, unfold the postcard and carefully cut along the dotted line shown below. Make sure that you don't cut through the two end strips.

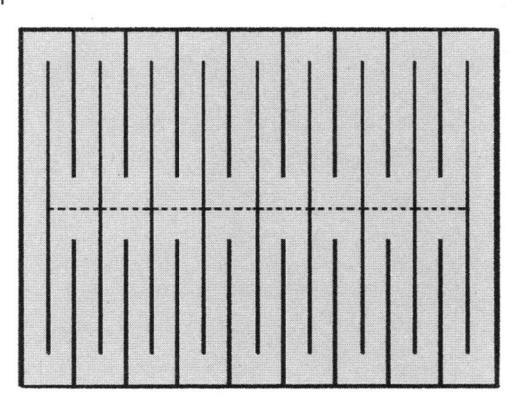

Finally, gently pull on the ends of the postcard and you will find that it forms a large chain of connected strips. Now you can easily place it over your head!

HARRY HOUDINI

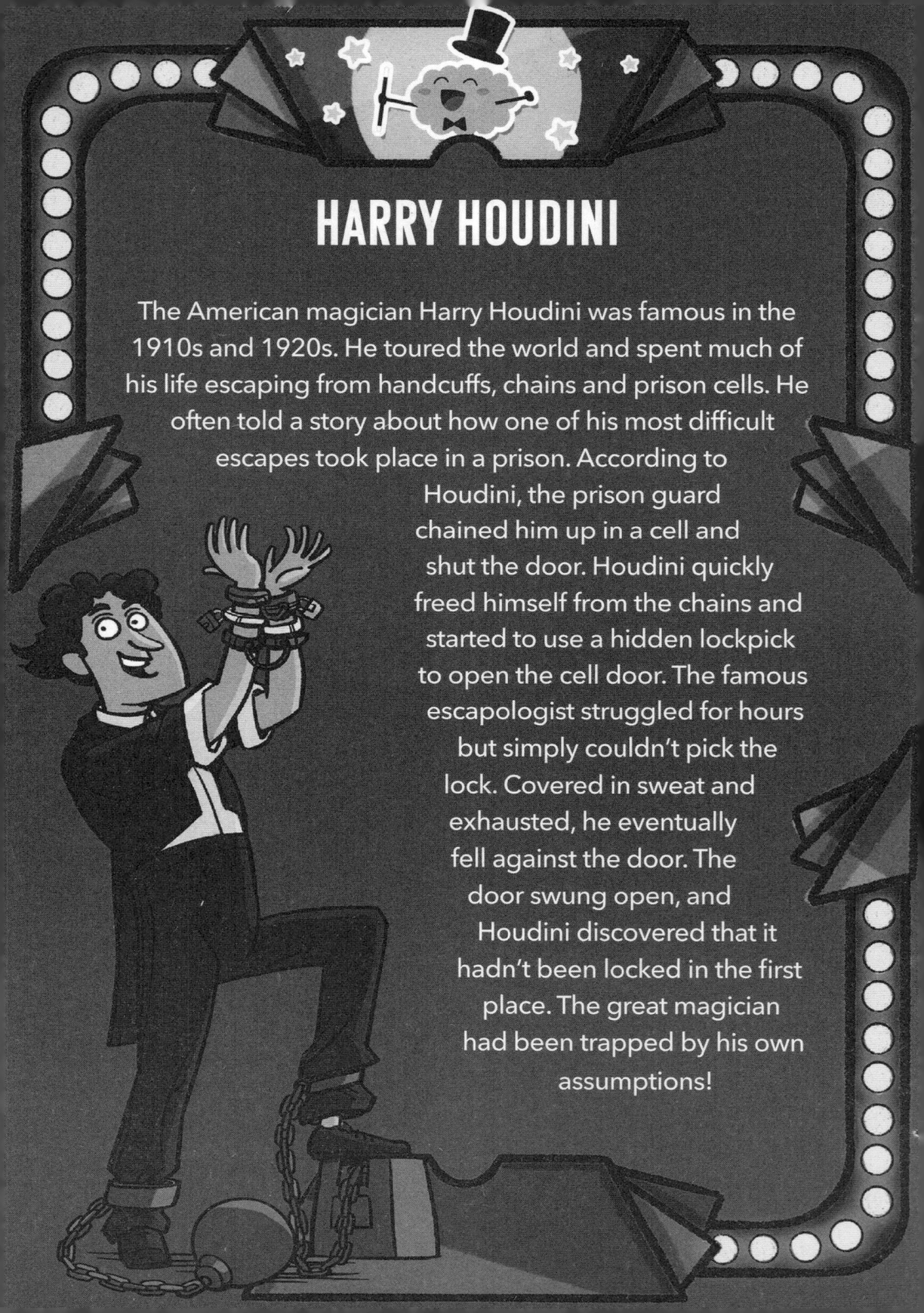

The American magician Harry Houdini was famous in the 1910s and 1920s. He toured the world and spent much of his life escaping from handcuffs, chains and prison cells. He often told a story about how one of his most difficult escapes took place in a prison. According to Houdini, the prison guard chained him up in a cell and shut the door. Houdini quickly freed himself from the chains and started to use a hidden lockpick to open the cell door. The famous escapologist struggled for hours but simply couldn't pick the lock. Covered in sweat and exhausted, he eventually fell against the door. The door swung open, and Houdini discovered that it hadn't been locked in the first place. The great magician had been trapped by his own assumptions!

This type of thinking is essential to creating magic tricks. Let's come up with a seemingly impossible idea and then figure out how we can make it happen!

THE PREDICTION

Imagine showing your friend a picture of a cat, a house and a tree, and asking them to choose one. Next, you reveal that you had already written down what they would do, correctly predicting their selection. That would be a great trick, but how can we do it?

Here's an idea. You could write 'I predict that you will choose the cat' on a piece of paper and put the paper in your pocket or bag. Then show your friend the pictures and hope that they choose the cat. The good news is that you will be correct about a third of the time. The bad news is that your prediction will be wrong whenever your friend chooses the house or tree.

Let's keep going. There is probably a better idea out there – we just haven't come up with it yet.

Let's imagine that your friend chooses the picture of the tree. You could put your hand in your pocket or bag, quickly write 'Tree' on a piece of paper and show them your prediction. Hmmm . . . good idea, but your friend might be suspicious about what's going on in your pocket or bag.

Ah, here's a thought. We are assuming that there is only one prediction, but what if there were several and you only showed your friend the correct one? That sounds promising, so let's think about how it might work. How about this . . .

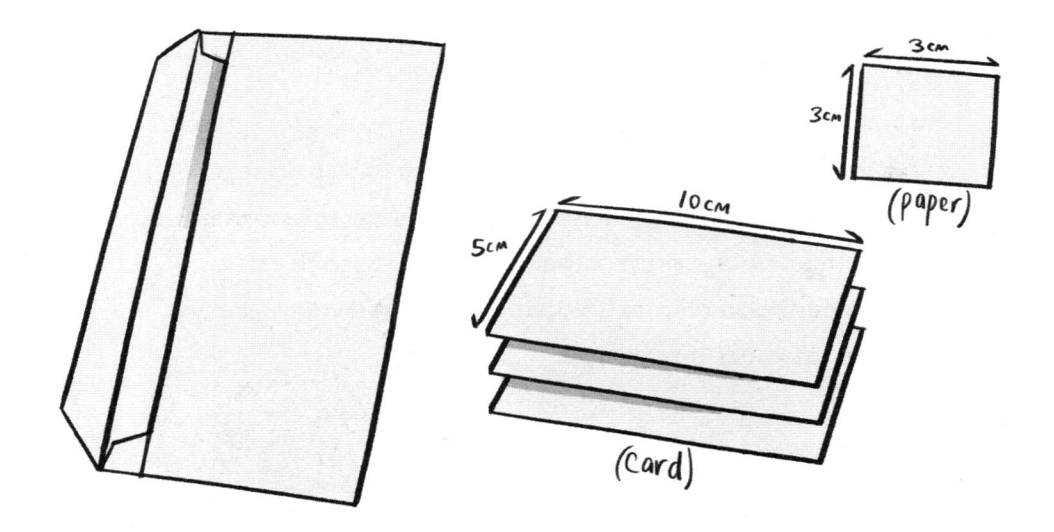

To perform this trick, you will need an envelope, three pieces of thin cardboard that are about 10 cm by 5 cm, and a small piece of paper that is about 3 cm by 3 cm. Before you begin, there are a few things you need to do.

First of all, draw a picture of a cat on one piece of thin card, a house on another and a tree on the final piece. This isn't a test of your artistic ability, so it's fine if your drawings aren't very good. Mine are terrible.

Then on the other side of the cat picture, write 'I predict that you will choose the cat'; on the small piece of paper write 'I predict that you will choose the house'; and on the front of the envelope write 'I predict that you will choose the tree'. Third, place the small piece of paper and the three pieces of cardboard inside the envelope.

Finally, put the envelope inside your pocket or bag.

To perform the trick, take the envelope out from your pocket or bag, being careful not to show the front. Now remove the three pieces of cardboard from the envelope and leave the small piece of paper inside. Place the envelope, front down, on the table and arrange the three pieces of cardboard in a line. Ask your friend to choose one of the pictures.

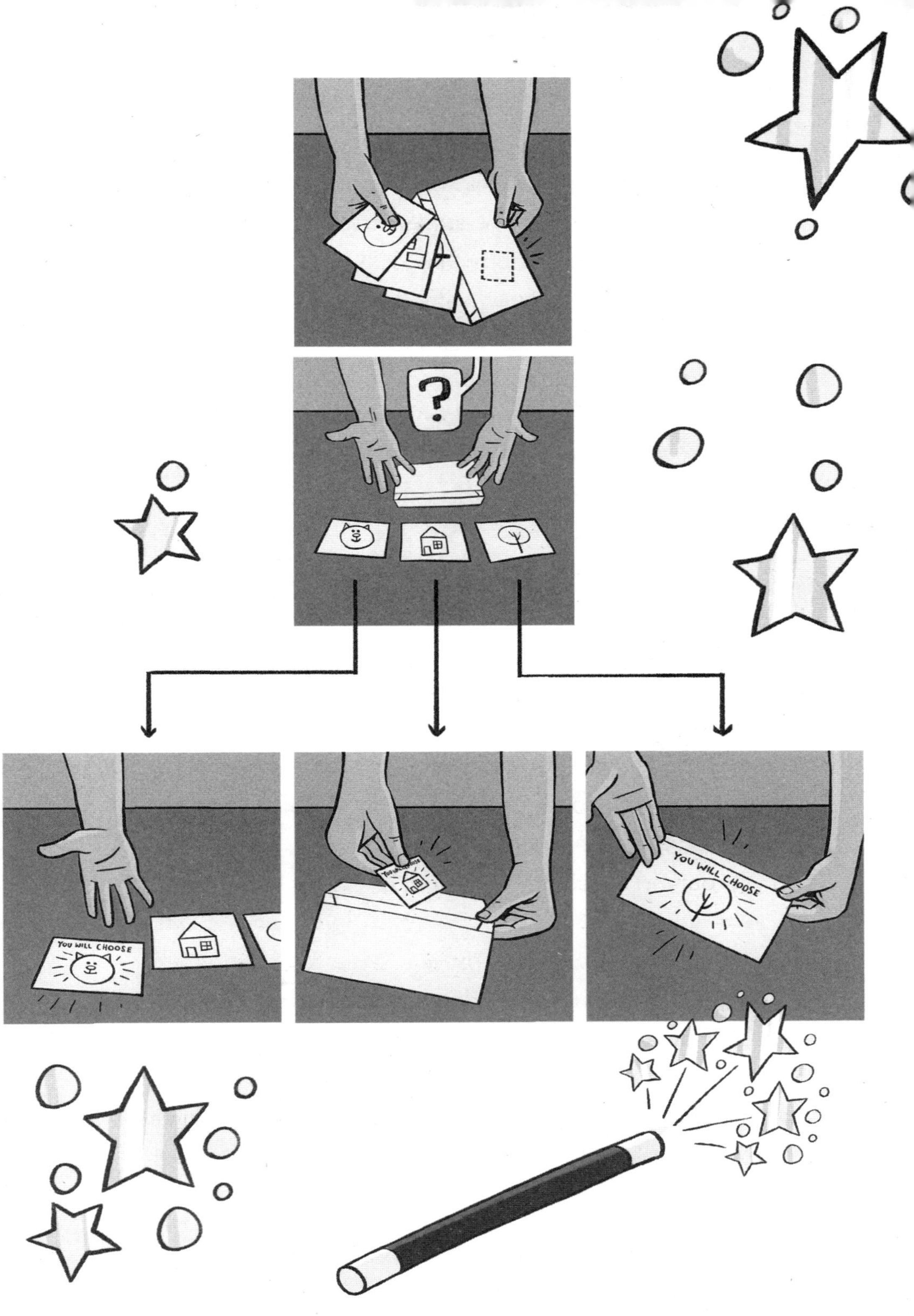
?
YOU WILL CHOOSE
YOU WILL CHOOSE
YOU WILL CHOOSE

At this point you can have some fun by acting as if you are trying to get your friend to choose a certain picture. For instance, you might say something like, *'This is a completely free choice,'* and then push the house picture forward, as if you want them to pick that one. Or maybe you could say, *'This is a perfectly tree . . . I mean free . . . choice.'* Eventually, your friend will choose a picture. Make sure that they are happy with their decision and tell them that it's fine if they want to change their mind.

What happens next depends on the picture that they selected . . .

If they chose the house, say something like, *'That's very strange. Last night I had an odd feeling and so I wrote something on this piece of paper.'* Then take the piece of paper out of the envelope and show that it says: 'I predict that you will choose the house'.

If your friend chose the cat, say, *'That's very strange. Last night, I had an odd feeling and so I wrote something on the back of one card.'* Then turn over all three cards to reveal that the cat card says: 'I predict that you will choose the cat'.

And if your friend chose the tree, say, *'That's very strange. Last night, I had an odd feeling and so I wrote something on the front of the envelope.'* Then turn the envelope over to show that it says: 'I predict that you will choose the tree'.

Whichever picture your friend chooses, your prediction will be correct! Your friends will be fooled by the trick because they'll assume that there is only one prediction. We did it!

The Prediction involved a picture of a tree, a house and a cat. But there are lots of other ways of presenting the illusion. You could draw a glass of cola, lemonade and orange juice, and ask your friend to choose a drink, or have photographs of a beach, a city and some mountains, and predict your friend's dream holiday. Perhaps you could perform the illusion with Top Trumps cards, or names for a pet, or colours, or famous people. Try thinking about other ways of presenting the trick and see which one you like best.

In everyday life you will face lots of tricky challenges. Maybe you want to become a famous musician or go to university. Perhaps you would like to find a way of helping people who are ill or creating videos that get millions of views online.

No matter the challenge, **believe that these things might be possible**, **dare to be different** and **have fun** finding a new way forward.

Think like a magician and see if you can make your dreams come true!

- Discover how other people have achieved similar goals
- Relax
- Take a break
- Challenge assumptions
- Have a shower
- Do the opposite to everyone else
- Sleep on it
- Come up with lots of ideas!

SUPERPOWER 3

MAKE FRIENDSHIPS APPEAR

Magic is a wonderful way of meeting people and making friends because it gives you something to say and do when you are with others. Lots of the tricks and challenges that we have already learned are great for this. If you are at a party, for example, you can make a person's finger stick to the table, show them a rubber band that jumps across your hand, challenge them to tie a knot in a piece of string without letting go of the ends and predict the future!

Here are a few more of my favourite party pieces that are perfect for putting a smile on people's faces and getting them chatting.

THE MYSTERIOUS NAPKIN

This illusion requires a paper or cloth napkin.

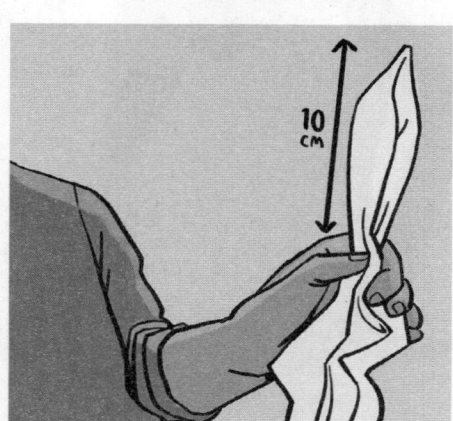

Hold your left hand vertically. Now place one corner of the napkin across your fingers, making sure that about 10 cm of it sticks out above your hand.

Gently grasp the napkin between your left thumb and your left first and second fingers.

Using your right hand, pretend to wrap an invisible piece of thread around the corner of the napkin. Now mime pulling the thread to your right.

As you pretend to pull the imaginary thread, gently press your left thumb against your first and second fingers. The corner of the napkin will bend over as if it's being pulled by the invisible thread!

Then pretend to let go of the invisible thread and release some of the pressure with your left thumb. The corner of the napkin will stand up straight again.

You might need to practise for a while to get the movement of your right hand matching the movement of the napkin, but once you have learned it, you can perform it anywhere!

THE ZOMBIE'S FINGER

This is more of a practical joke than a trick, but it's great for getting people talking.

You will need a cardboard box that has a loose-fitting lid and is about 10 cm long, about 7 cm wide and about 3 cm deep. If you have small hands, then you can use a smaller box. Carefully cut a hole in the bottom of the box, towards one end, making sure that it is slightly larger than your second finger. Now stick a thin layer of cotton wool inside the box – but don't cover the gap – and use a red marker pen to colour around the edges of the hole.

To perform this illusion, take out the box from your pocket or bag. Do not show your friend the hole in the bottom. Place the box on to your left hand, and hold it in place with your left thumb, and third and little fingers. As you put the box on your hand, secretly push your second finger into the hole, bend it over and lay it flat against the cotton wool. Say that you have a strange souvenir of a recent zombie attack.

Then remove the lid and show that the box contains a zombie's finger! Move your finger a little bit and it will seem to come alive!

This illusion can be slightly scary so it's best to present it in a light-hearted way.

As this is more of a joke than a magic trick, it's fine to reveal the secret and even let people try it for themselves.

WHAT'S THAT BEHIND YOUR EAR?

This is a classic magic trick which involves producing a coin from behind a person's ear.

First, you need to learn how to hide a coin in your hand. Find a coin that is about the same width as your two middle fingers.

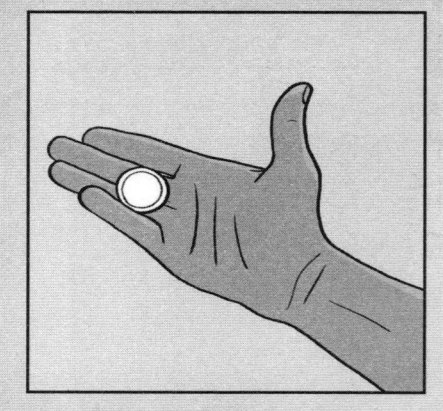

Put the coin at the bottom of the two middle fingers of your dominant hand. Then curl your fingers inwards, so that the coin is gently held between the base and the first joints of the fingers.

Practise holding a coin like that until it feels comfortable and you can walk around without the coin falling out.

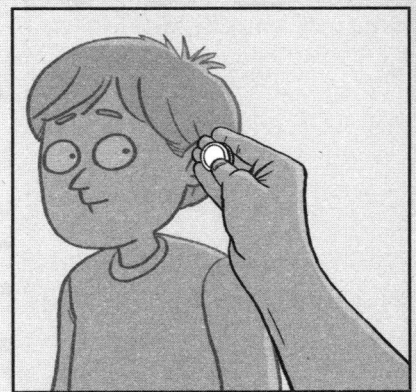

Just before you perform this illusion, sneakily put a coin into this secret position. When you are with your friend, use your other hand to point behind their ear and say something like, *'What's that behind your ear?'*

Move the hand that is holding the coin behind their ear and use your thumb to slide the coin towards your fingertips.

Finally, show them your hand, holding the coin!

THE FLOATING CUP

You will need an empty disposable paper cup for this trick.

Before you perform this illusion, carefully tear a small hole about the size of your thumb in the side of the empty paper cup, close to the bottom.

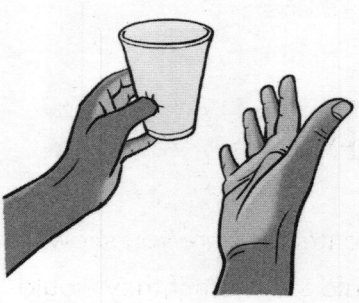

When you are with a friend, secretly put your thumb into the hole, then spread out your fingers and raise your hand.

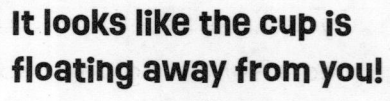

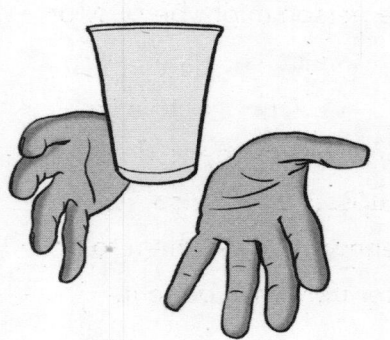

It looks like the cup is floating away from you!

This is a good exercise in acting. Hold your other hand next to the cup, and then close both hands around it so it will look like you've caught it just before it floated too high and got away.

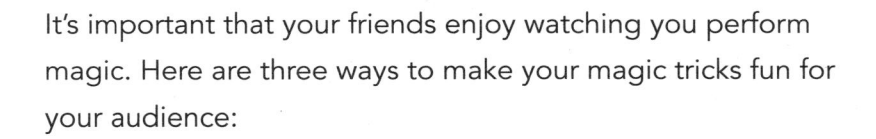

It's important that your friends enjoy watching you perform magic. Here are three ways to make your magic tricks fun for your audience:

1 BE POLITE

- Everyone likes to be treated politely. Before you show someone some magic, you could ask them if they would like to see a trick. After all, the person might be busy or dislike watching magic!

- When you are performing, don't ask anyone to do anything that embarrasses or upsets them. Also, remember to say 'please' whenever you ask them to do something and 'thank you' after they have done it.

- If someone makes a mistake when they are helping you during a trick, say something like, *'Oh that often happens. Don't worry about it.'* Or, *'That's OK, I probably didn't explain that very clearly.'*

- Finally, if your friend offers to show you a trick, be a good audience for them, in the same way that you want them to be a good audience for you.

2 ENJOY YOURSELF

Emotions are like coughs and colds – we can catch them from one another! **If you enjoy yourself when you perform magic, your friends will catch your positive mood.** That's important because most of us like to be around people who make us feel good.

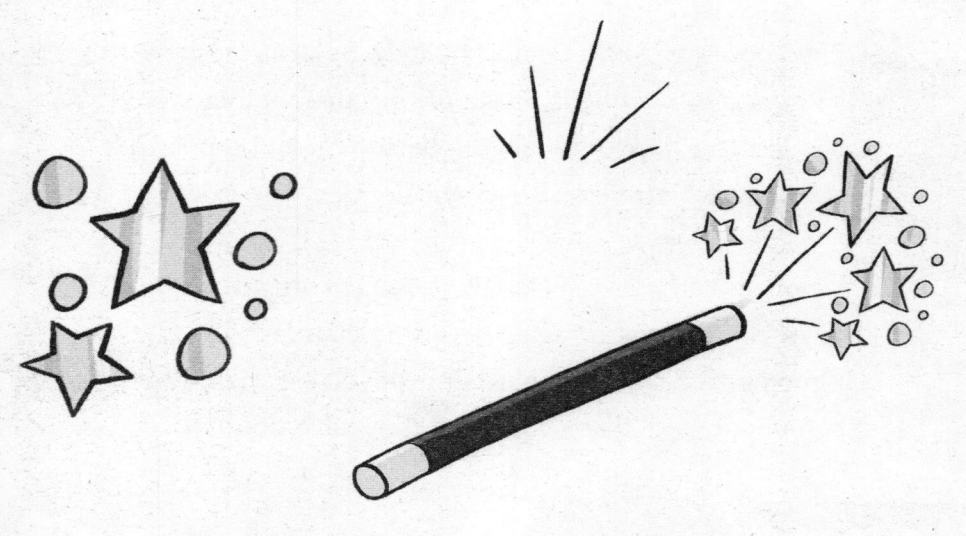

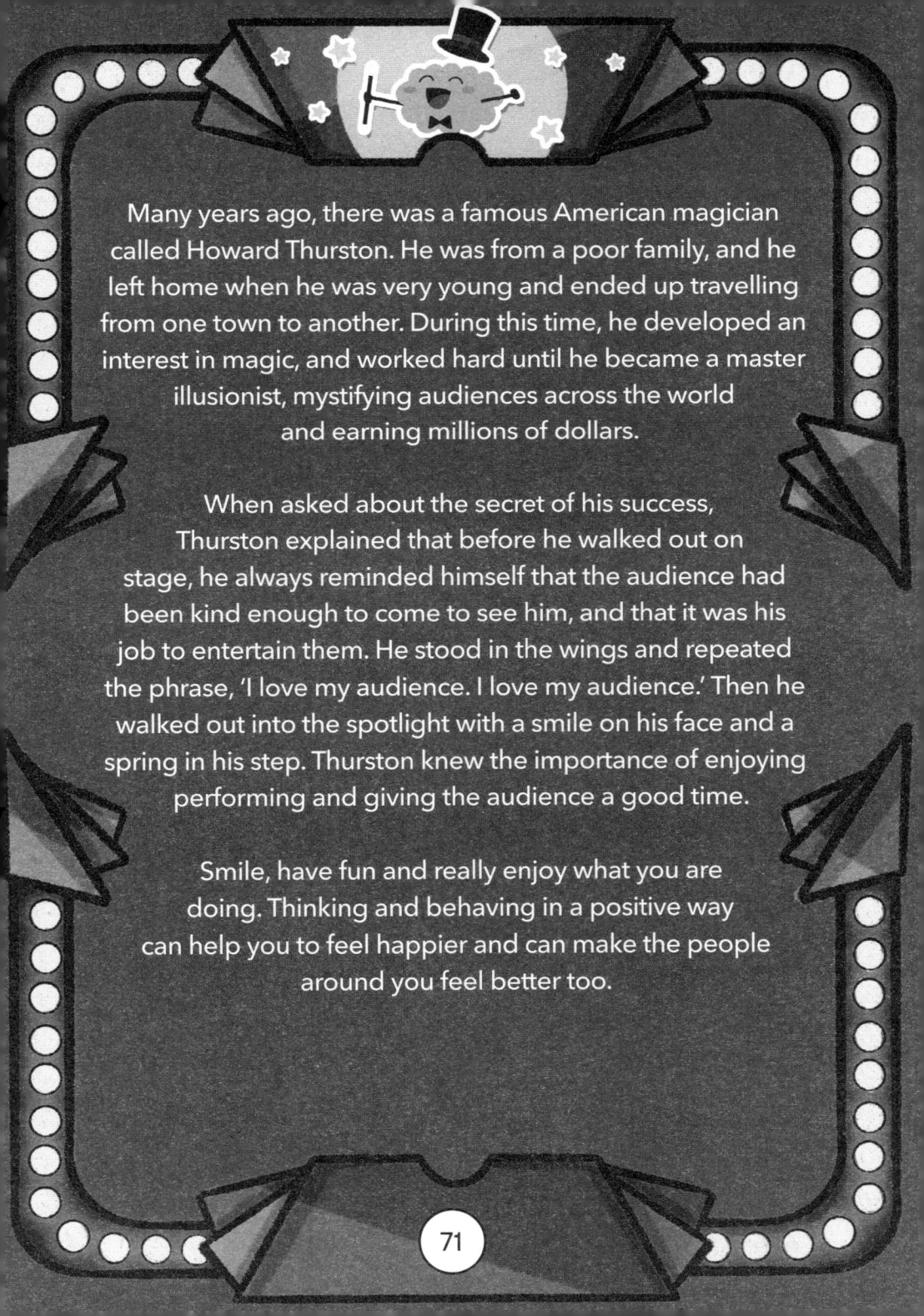

Many years ago, there was a famous American magician called Howard Thurston. He was from a poor family, and he left home when he was very young and ended up travelling from one town to another. During this time, he developed an interest in magic, and worked hard until he became a master illusionist, mystifying audiences across the world and earning millions of dollars.

When asked about the secret of his success, Thurston explained that before he walked out on stage, he always reminded himself that the audience had been kind enough to come to see him, and that it was his job to entertain them. He stood in the wings and repeated the phrase, 'I love my audience. I love my audience.' Then he walked out into the spotlight with a smile on his face and a spring in his step. Thurston knew the importance of enjoying performing and giving the audience a good time.

Smile, have fun and really enjoy what you are doing. Thinking and behaving in a positive way can help you to feel happier and can make the people around you feel better too.

3 SHARE THE SPOTLIGHT

Have you ever met someone who talks only about themselves? Some people want to show off and to always be the **centre of attention**. That's not much fun to watch. **Your magic will be at its best when you involve and include your friends.**

One of the most powerful ways of doing this is to let them do the magic. Do you remember when you made a band magically jump across your hand? When you first learned this, I suggested that you say the word 'jump' as you opened your fingers. But how about getting your friends to say 'jump' and making the band move at their command? That way, you have **shared the spotlight**.

FOUR SUMS

My friend Marlies Greve lives in the Netherlands and is the president of a wonderful organisation called Magic Care. Marlies and other magicians regularly visit hospitals and teach magic to children who aren't very well. The magic brightens their day and makes them feel better. Marlies has come up with a lovely idea that I wanted to show you. What do you notice about these four sums?

$$2 + 2 = 4$$
$$3 + 6 = 9$$
$$4 + 2 = 8$$
$$2 + 1 = 3$$

Almost everyone notices that the third sum is wrong, and hardly anyone says that the other three are correct. That's because we all tend to **notice what's wrong, rather than what's right**. It's the same in our everyday lives. When we talk to our friends and family, we frequently criticise rather than compliment. That's unfortunate because we all love to receive genuine compliments. **When you meet someone, focus on what you like about them and what they do well.**

Let's put all these ideas together and . . .

DRUM ROLL

. . . perform your very first card trick!

YOU ARE ACE!

Magicians have invented lots of complicated tricks with cards, but let's start with something simple (remember, one step at a time!). Your helper is going to do most of the work for you, so it's best to choose someone who can pick up and deal cards.

Before you start, let's get to know your cards. A full deck contains 52 cards, although many of the tricks in this book will work even if some of the cards are missing. There are four suits. Two of them are red (Diamonds and Hearts) and two of them are black (Spades and Clubs). Within each suit, there are thirteen cards that go from Ace to Ten, plus the Jack, Queen and King. Some decks also have one or two Jokers as extra cards. The side of the card showing the value and suit is called the face and the other side is called the back. Welcome to your cards!

Now, back to the trick. Put the four Aces face-down on top of the deck. When you start, say something like, *'Let's see if you can use your magical powers to do something amazing.'*

Place the deck of cards face-down on the table, and ask your friend to divide the deck in half and place the upper section on your right.

Then have them divide the left pile roughly in half and put the upper section to your left. Now ask them to divide the right pile roughly in half and to put the upper section to your right. That way, there will be four piles in a row, and the pile on your far right will have the four Aces on top of it.

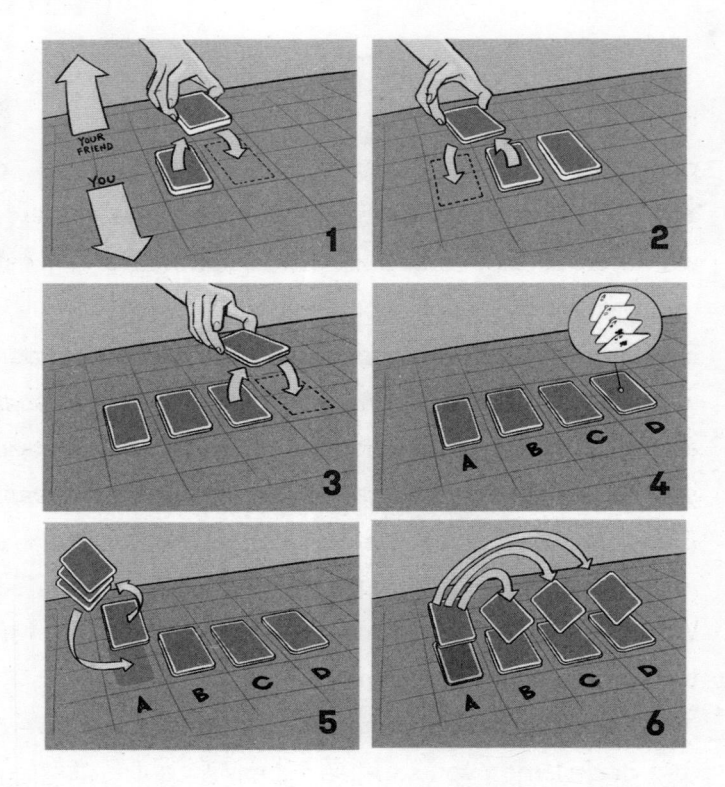

Explain that your friend is going to mix up the cards in a strange way. Point to the pile on your far left, and ask your friend to pick it up and move the top three cards from the top of the pile to the bottom of the pile. Next, ask them to deal a card from the top of their pile on to each of the piles on the table. Finally, ask them to place the pile back in its original position on the table.

Then, moving along the row, point to the next pile and politely ask them to carry out the same moves. Again, three cards are moved from the top of the pile to the bottom of the pile, a card is dealt on to each of the piles on the table, and the pile is then returned to the table.

Now move along the row again, point to the third pile and politely ask them to carry out the moves again. Finally, ask them to carry out the same moves with the pile on the far right (which contains the Aces).

Explain that your friend could have divided the cards anywhere, and that they have mixed up the cards again and again. Then say something like, *'Wouldn't it be amazing if you had used your magical powers without even realising it? Please look at the four top cards.'*

When your friend turns over the cards on the top of each pile, they will discover the four Aces!

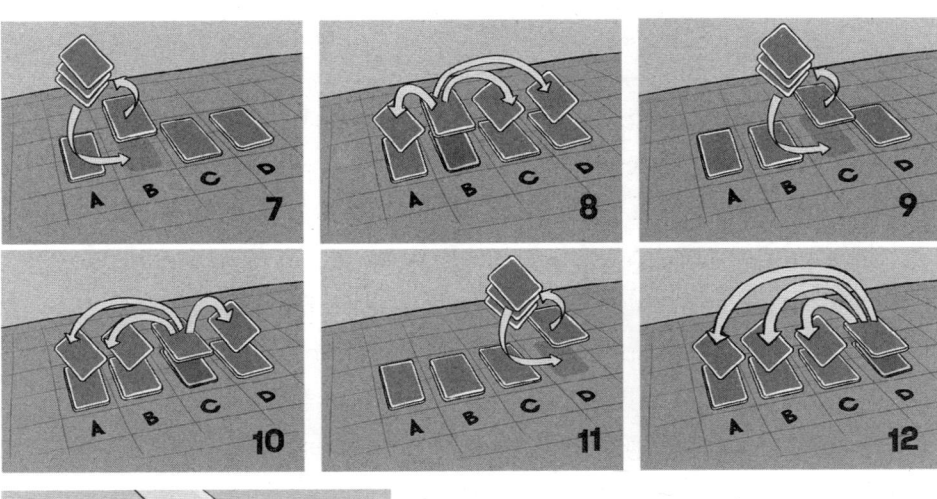

This trick was first published by Steve Belchou in 1939.

To make this trick as entertaining as possible, be enthusiastic and enjoy yourself. Pretend that you have never done this before and are interested in what is happening. Remember to say 'please' and 'thank you' when your friend helps you.

Most important of all, celebrate their success and congratulate them on finding the Aces. Make it about them, not you.

The ability to imagine how someone else feels is called **empathy**, and it's an important skill in magic. To develop empathy, **think about what would make someone else feel happy**. If you were watching a magician, would you like to see a performer who enjoys what they are doing, says 'please' and 'thank you', and shares the attention with other people? **Be that magician** and you will find it easy to entertain other people.

The same ideas apply in everyday life. We like people who are polite and respectful, and who make us feel good. Most important of all, we like people who are interested in us. I am a big fan of a writer called Dale Carnegie. He wrote a wonderful book called *How to Win Friends and Influence People*, and I read it when I was about twelve years old. It is full of great advice. At one point Carnegie explains that you will make more friends in ten minutes by being genuinely interested in other people than in ten years of trying to make them interested in you. When you are talking to people, don't make it all about you. Ask them about themselves and listen to what they say.

Make them the star of the show.

To make friends by magic:

- Be positive
- Be polite
- Be interested in other people!

SUPERPOWER 4

MASTER MAGICAL TEAMWORK

Teamwork is really important in everyday life. Although we can achieve lots on our own, **working with other people is often fun** and more productive. Let's discover how to be a great team player by magic.

Imagine seeing an impressive magic show. At the end of the performance, the master magician takes their bow as the audience clap and cheer. It's easy to think that the performer created everything that you have seen. In fact, most big shows involve a large team of people, including those who invent illusions, write scripts, design scenery, compose music, work the lighting and sound, and carry out secret stuff backstage.

Even the seemingly simplest of tricks can involve teamwork, and magicians have been working with others for a very long time.

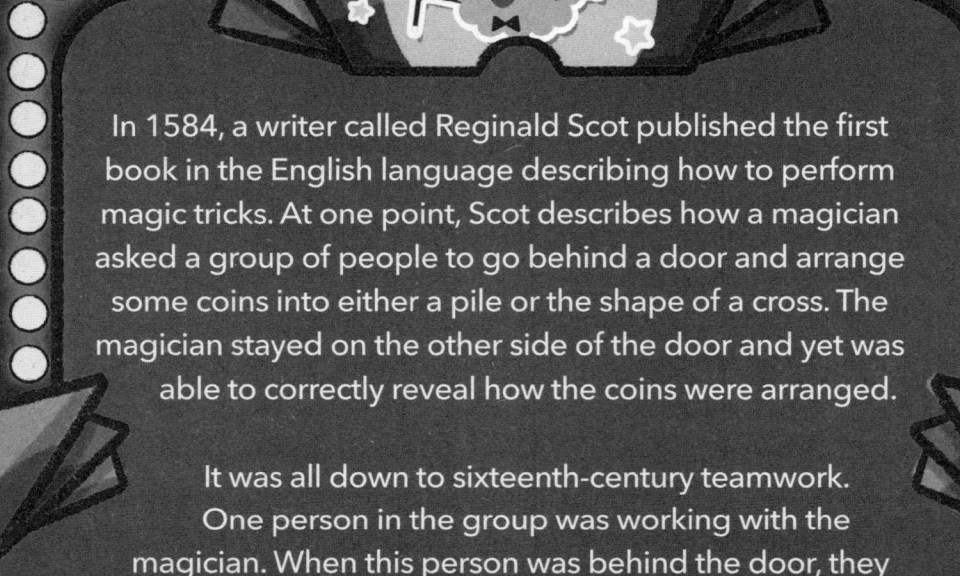

In 1584, a writer called Reginald Scot published the first book in the English language describing how to perform magic tricks. At one point, Scot describes how a magician asked a group of people to go behind a door and arrange some coins into either a pile or the shape of a cross. The magician stayed on the other side of the door and yet was able to correctly reveal how the coins were arranged.

It was all down to sixteenth-century teamwork. One person in the group was working with the magician. When this person was behind the door, they used a secret code. If the coins had been arranged in the shape of a cross, the person asked the magician, 'What is it?' but if the coins had been put into a pile, the person said, 'What ist?' which is an old-fashioned way of asking the same question.

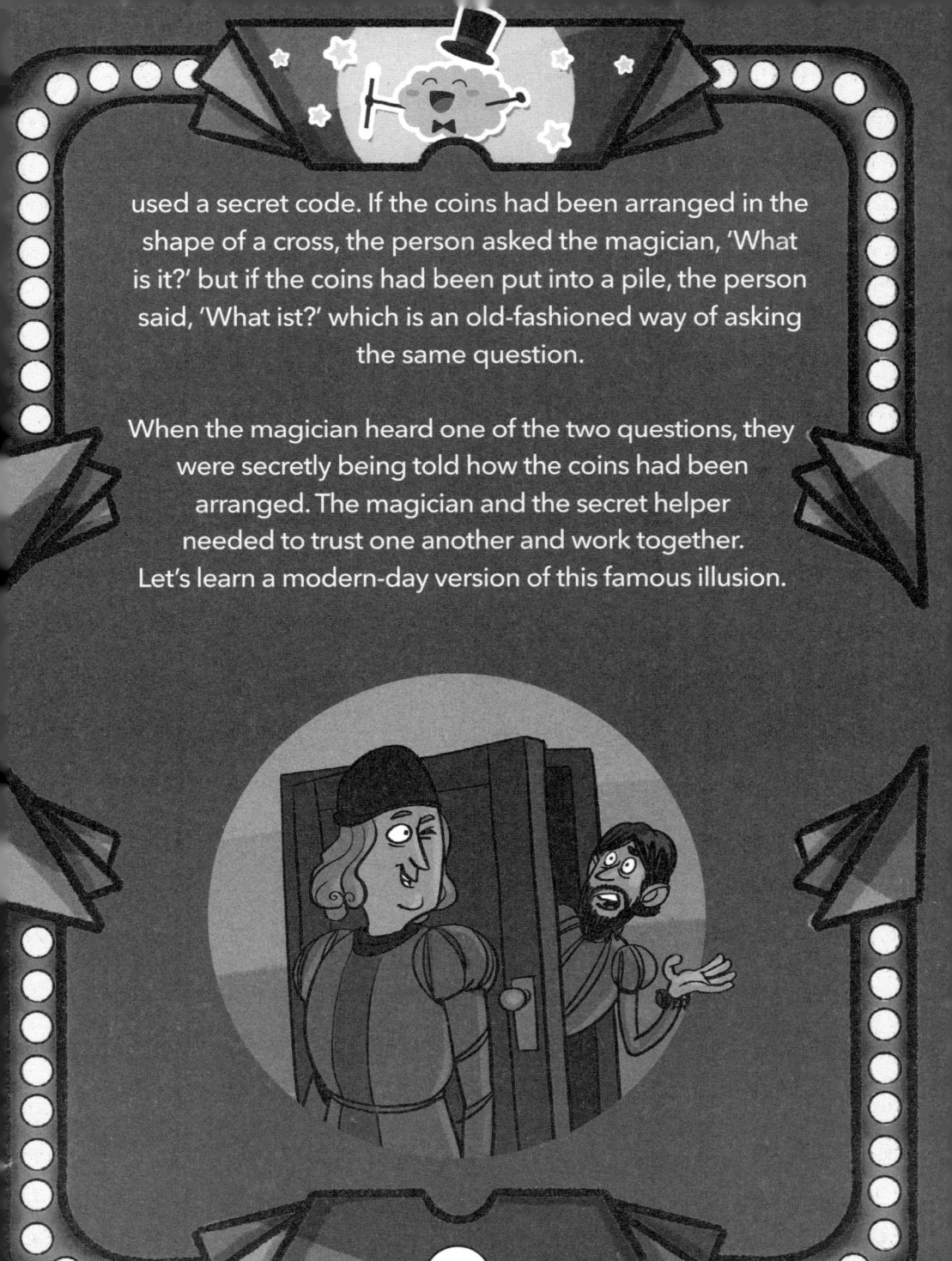

When the magician heard one of the two questions, they were secretly being told how the coins had been arranged. The magician and the secret helper needed to trust one another and work together. Let's learn a modern-day version of this famous illusion.

FIVE IN A ROW

Performing this illusion is fun and easy. This trick is best performed for a group of your friends or family. Begin by asking them to collect any five objects and then arrange them in a row on a table. Next, explain that you will leave the room for a few minutes, and that while you are away, the group needs to select one. When you return to the room, ask them to think about the chosen object. Amazingly, you can correctly name which item they selected!

Like the classic illusion described by Reginald Scot over four hundred years ago, this trick involves a secret helper. Before you start, quietly ask someone in the group if they are willing to help you during the illusion. Try to choose someone who is reliable and won't be suspected by the other people in the group.

Tell your helper that there will be five objects in a line on the table. Let's imagine that the line looks like this . . .

SHOE   SMARTPHONE   BALL   SPOON   WATCH

Next, ask your secret helper to imagine numbering the objects from one to five, starting with the one on their left. In our example, the objects would be numbered like this . . .

1. SHOE　　**2. SMARTPHONE**　　**3. BALL**　　**4. SPOON**　　**5. WATCH**

Explain that the group will choose one of the objects and that your helper needs to secretly signal which one has been selected. The signal is very simple and involves holding out the fingers and thumb of their right hand.

For instance, if the SHOE (object number one) is chosen, your helper holds out one finger; if the BALL (object number three) is chosen, they hold out three fingers; and if the WATCH (object number five) is chosen, they hold out four fingers and their thumb.

Your helper needs to make the signal clear, but not so obvious that the other people in the group notice it. They might find it helpful to keep their hand on their lap or down by their side. When you come back into the room, quickly glance at your helper's hand and use the code to figure out which object has been chosen. Ask the group to think really hard about the item they picked and then dramatically reveal their selection.

For the trick to be a success, you and your helper need to **work together**. You both make an important contribution, and the illusion only works if you each do your bit.

Remember that when the trick succeeds, it's thanks to the two of you being **a great team**. Similarly, if something goes wrong, try not to blame one another, and instead sort out the issue by working together. When you are in a team, it's often useful to **understand everyone's contribution**, and swapping roles is a great way of doing this. Another time, your helper could try performing the trick and you could send them the secret signal.

Like most magic tricks, this illusion can be presented in different ways. For instance, you could make it more entertaining by pretending to look into someone's mind and then saying something funny like . . .

'In your mind you have a picture of a giant purple dog wearing a bright yellow party hat . . . That's odd . . . why are you thinking of that? Oh, hold on, the dog has something in its mouth . . . It's the ball!'

You can also experiment with different codes. For instance, you could ask the group to choose a person, rather than an object, and have your helper signal the chosen person by copying how they are sitting or standing. If the chosen person is sitting down with their legs and arms crossed, for example, then your helper does the same. If they are standing up with their arms down by their sides, your helper copies that.

THE VANISHING COIN

Let's use teamwork to make a coin disappear. You will need a small coin and a handkerchief or any similar-sized piece of cloth.

This trick is performed to a group of four or five people. Everyone can be sitting down but it's easier if they are standing up. One of them is your **secret helper**.

Hold up the palm of your left hand and place the coin on it. Show everyone the coin and then cover your hand with the cloth. Working your way around the group, ask everyone to place their hands under the cloth and check that the coin is still there by touching it. Make sure that your helper is the last person that you choose.

When your helper places their hands under the cloth, they secretly pick up the coin and hide it in their hand. Pretend to still have the coin in your left hand and move away from your helper. Your helper should put their hand, holding the hidden coin, down by their side.

The group will think that the coin is still under the cloth. Now say a **magic word** and throw the cloth into the air to reveal that the coin has vanished. While everyone is clapping and cheering, your helper can quietly put the coin into their pocket or bag.

Like any good trick, this requires practice. You and your helper need to **practise** the illusion so that you can perform it smoothly. Make sure that your friend can secretly remove the coin without it looking suspicious or knocking the handkerchief out of position.

This trick can be performed with any small object that your secret helper can hide in their hand. What else could you use?

IS THIS IT?

Another type of teamwork involves forming a double act with a second performer. For instance, for over fifty years the husband-and-wife act Goldfinger and Dove performed on stages around the world. Working to high-energy music, they plucked a seemingly endless stream of playing cards from thin air and danced with a floating cane. Similarly, for many years the famous magicians Siegfried and Roy performed their spectacular magic show in Las Vegas. Each night, they levitated high above the stage and even battled a giant fire-breathing dragon!

One of my favourite double acts were The Piddingtons. Sydney Piddington was a soldier during the Second World War. He was sent to fight in Singapore but was captured and spent three years in a Japanese prisoner-of-war camp. Sydney entertained his fellow inmates with mind reading and other amazing stunts. Following the war, Sydney married an actress named Lesley, and they created an amazing act in which Lesley appeared to receive Sydney's thoughts. She seemed to know what her husband was thinking, even when she was underwater in a diving bell, locked up in the Tower of London or flying in an aeroplane thousands of feet above the Earth.

Like all good magicians, The Piddingtons never revealed how they achieved their amazing feats. However, you and a friend can perform your own version of their wonderful double act.

THE MIND READER

This is another trick that you can show to a group of people. You and your friend explain that you seem to have an amazing connection. You often wear the same clothes and finish each other's sentences, and neither of you likes going to the dentist. Your friend then leaves the room for a few minutes, and while they are away, the remaining people in the group choose an object. Let's imagine that it is the sofa.

Your friend returns and you walk around the room, pointing to objects. Each time you say, *'This . . .'* and your friend finishes the sentence by saying, *'. . . is not the object.'* But then you point to the sofa and say, *'This . . .'* and your friend says, *'. . . IS the object.'* The two of you have used your **amazing bond** to find the correct item.

Before you begin, you and your friend need to select an object in the room. Let's imagine that it's a clock. You then agree to point to the clock directly before you point to the object chosen by the group. When your friend sees you point at the clock, they'll know that the next object is the chosen one. But what happens if the group choose the clock? Agree that you will sit in silence instead of walking round the room pointing at objects. When your friend sees that you aren't walking around saying anything, they will know that the clock has been chosen.

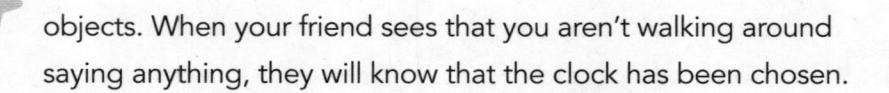

Once again, it's all down to **great teamwork**. Each of you plays an important role in the performance, and the two of you can swap roles to find out what it's like to be the other member of the team.

Once you and your friend have mastered this illusion, you can improve it. For instance, your friend could be the one sending you a signal. In this version you point to objects, and they say something like, *'No,'* or *'That's not it,'* or *'No, that's not the object.'* However, at one point they need to say, *'Nope.'* When you hear that signal, you point to the chosen object next. This version is more fooling because there doesn't seem to be any way you could be sending your friend a **secret code**.

Teamwork makes the dream work

In everyday life, it's important to be able to work with other people and to be a team player. This involves:
- Making sure that your contribution is the best that it can be
- Helping other team members
- Acknowledging that everyone's contribution is important and knowing that any success is the result of you all working together

I am a big fan of the late American television presenter Mister Rogers. He dedicated his life to creating a wonderful television programme that encouraged viewers to deal with difficult emotions, to be confident and to be kind to one another. Mister Rogers received lots of awards throughout his life and always thanked the team that was involved in making the programme a success.

He also had a wonderful way of reminding us that **we are all part of a team**. When he collected an award, Mister Rogers asked his audience to spend 60 seconds thinking about the people who had supported them and cared about them; the people who had believed in them, wanted what was best for them, helped them and made sacrifices for them. Maybe it was their family, or their friends, or their teachers, or their neighbours.

Let's try it right now. Please take a minute to think about the people who, as Mister Rogers put it, have 'loved you into being'.

> **Who did you think about?**
> **These people are your team.**
>
> **Life is about working together and being part of a great team.**

** SURPRISE INTERMISSION **

You have discovered how to make a band jump across your fingers, read people's minds, produce a coin from behind your friend's ear and much more. Well done. This seems like a good time to take a quick break and discuss the three basic rules of magic.

RULE 1 – Try not to repeat an illusion
Your friends might ask you to perform a trick a second time, but it's best to resist the temptation to do so! If you perform the illusion again, your friends won't be surprised and might be able to figure out what's happening. Instead, show them another amazing trick.

RULE 2 – Less is more

Instead of trying to learn all the tricks in this book, it's better to focus on being able to perform a small number of them well. Similarly, rather than showing your friends and family lots of tricks, only perform one or two for them and leave it there. Like many things in life, quality is better than quantity.

RULE 3 – Resist the urge to reveal methods

It's best to keep magical secrets to yourself because telling people how a trick is done is often disappointing, makes it difficult for other magicians to perform the same trick and removes wonder from the world. Indeed, when magicians join a magic club, they often take an oath of secrecy. If someone asks, *'How did you do that?'* you could politely say something like, *'It took lots of practice,'* or, *'I have no idea – it always happens like that,'* or simply, *'It's magic!'*

As with most rules, however, there are exceptions . . .

Let's imagine that you meet someone who loves magic and really wants you to perform lots of tricks. Or that not revealing a secret to a good friend would mean losing their friendship. Or that someone is genuinely interested in magic, and teaching them a trick would encourage them to learn more about this amazing performing art. In these situations, it might be OK to break the rules.

Like many decisions in life, it's a matter of **doing what you think is right**. Magic is about making the world a better place. Remember that and you will usually know the right thing to do.

OK, ON WITH THE SHOW!

SUPERPOWER 5

ACE RESILIENCE

It would be great if everything in life worked out well. However, occasionally you will make a mistake or encounter a setback. The good news is that magicians have lots of ways of dealing with these tricky situations. Let's discover how they transform failure into success, and how you can use these skills in everyday life.

When I started out in magic, one of my favourite tricks involved reaching inside a seemingly empty black bag and dramatically producing an egg. The trick was easy to do because the egg was hidden in a secret pocket inside the bag. One day my teacher asked me to perform some magic for my classmates and I decided to begin with the egg trick. I showed everyone the apparently empty bag and then placed my hand inside. Unfortunately, I couldn't find the egg. I felt around and eventually I discovered that the egg had broken. Worse still, my fingers were now covered in a smelly eggy mess. I vividly remember explaining that the trick had gone wrong and having to perform the rest of the show with a sticky yellow hand!

Every magician will tell you similar stories. No matter how much you practise, **tricks sometimes go wrong**. The good news is that you can always have a plan to deal with setbacks. Let's find out more with the help of another great card trick.

IS THIS YOUR CARD?

For this trick you need a deck of cards. It doesn't matter if a few of them are missing. Before you begin, secretly look at the card on the bottom of the deck and remember it. Let's imagine that it's the Ace of Clubs.

At the start of the trick, ask your friend to take any card out of the middle of the deck and look at it without showing you. Now place the deck face-down on a table and have your friend put their card face-down on top of the deck. Ask your friend to divide the deck by picking up about half the cards from the top and placing them face-down on the table. Finally, ask them to pick up the remaining cards and place them on top of the rest so the deck is complete.

Your friend won't realise it, but the Ace of Clubs is now on top of their card. Ask your friend to divide the deck and then place the remaining cards on top, as many times as they like. No matter how often they do that, their card will still be directly below the Ace of Clubs.

Now it's time for you to find their card. Take the card that is on the top of the deck and place it, face up, on to the table. Then do the same with the second card, then the third card, and so on as you go through the deck. At some point, you will see the Ace of Clubs. When this happens, pick up the next card and say, 'I think this is your card.' Ask your friend to tell you the name of the card they chose, then turn the card over to show that you are correct.

There is one exception to this. If your friend happens to divide the cards between the Ace of Clubs and their chosen card, then Ace of Clubs will be on the bottom of the deck and the chosen card will be on the top. If that happens, the Ace of Clubs will be the last card that you turn over. When you finally see the Ace of Clubs, say something like, *'Ah, I think your card was the very first one that I put on the table.'* Then show your friend the first card that you turned over and you will be correct.

There are lots of ways of presenting this illusion to make it more fun. For instance, you could explain that people unconsciously wiggle their nose when they see their card, and then pretend to look at your friend's nose after you have shown them each card. Once you have placed their card on the table, you could say something like, *'Ah, the end of your nose just moved, that must be your card!'*

Or you could turn your friend's card over and place it face-up on the table. Then pick up the next card, hold it face-down and say, *'Your card will be the next one that I turn over.'* Your friend won't believe you because their card is already on the table. But you can then put the card you are holding down and pick up their chosen card from the table and turn it over so that it is face-down!

We can use this trick to explore the three things that magicians do to deal with setbacks. Let's take these one at a time.

1 LOOK FOR SOLUTIONS, NOT PROBLEMS

Magicians think about what might go wrong and what can be done to try to avoid this happening. There's no point in worrying about a space alien suddenly arriving from Mars and spoiling the card trick, because that's very unlikely to happen. Instead, they focus on things that are likely to go wrong. For instance, when it comes to the card trick, you might forget the card that was on the bottom of the deck. What can you do to help prevent this? Well, you could always put the same card on the bottom of the deck each time that you perform the trick. That way it's much easier to remember. Also, your friend might forget the card that they selected. Again, what can you do to prevent this happening? Well, if you

103

are performing for a group, you could ask your friend to show everyone their chosen card. That way, if they forget the card, someone else will probably remember it.

Finally, there might be some confusion when the selected card is returned to the deck. To help prevent this, keep your instructions clear, and watch what your friend is doing when they divide the cards and when they return their selected card to the deck.

Now let's move on to the second stage.

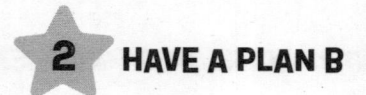

2   HAVE A PLAN B

Magicians often think about what they will do if the worst happens, and their trick goes wrong. This usually involves quickly switching to Plan B!

Let's imagine that you have forgotten the bottom card, or that you have lost track of it, or that you have revealed the wrong card. First, and most importantly, **don't panic!** Your friends didn't know what you were going to do and so they aren't aware that things are not going to plan.

Here's a helping hand that can fix everything (well, not everything, just this trick!).

On the next page there is an illustration containing all 52 cards. Carefully copy the illustration on to a sheet of paper or photocopy it, fold the paper in half and put it in your pocket or bag.

Ask your friend to name their card, then remove the piece of paper from your pocket or bag and say something like, 'It would be amazing if your card was on this piece of paper!'

Then unfold the paper, point to their card and say something like, 'All the cards are here . . . and there is your card!' You have turned the failure into a joke and saved the day. Now you can move on to another trick.

It was magician MacKenzie Gordon Gant who came up with the idea of using a picture of all 52 playing cards like this.

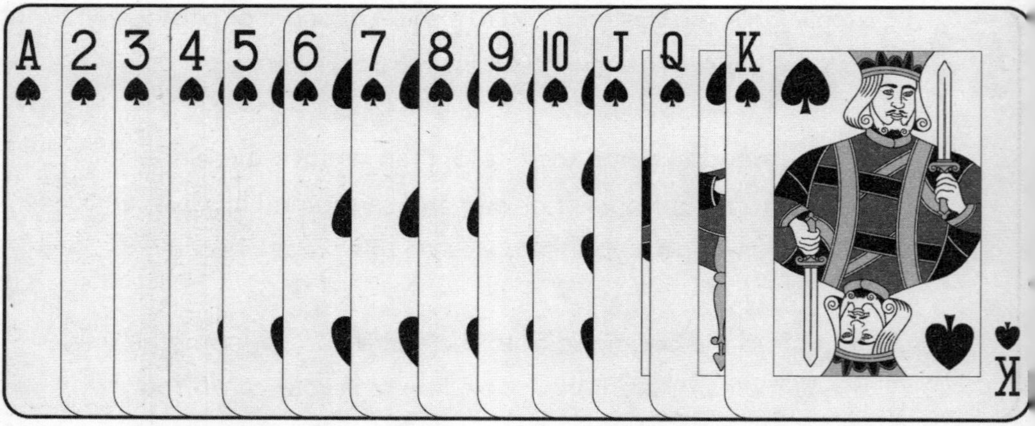
A 2 3 4 5 6 7 8 9 10 J Q K

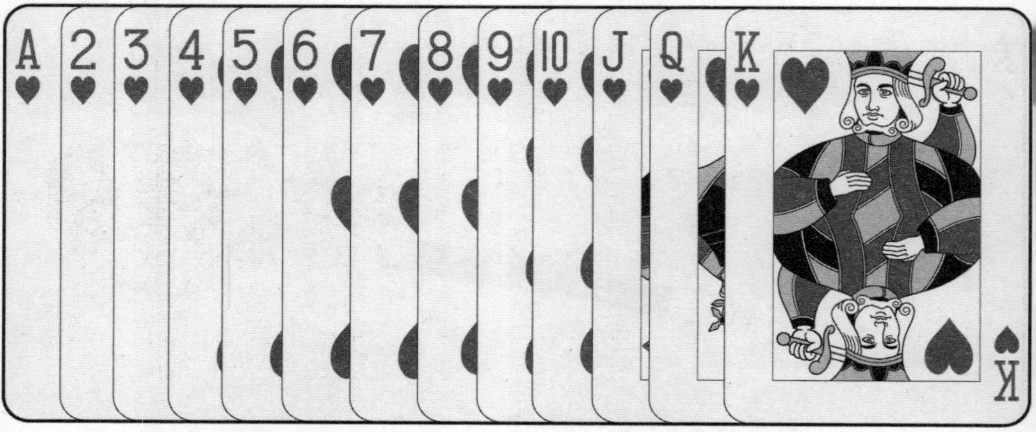
A 2 3 4 5 6 7 8 9 10 J Q K

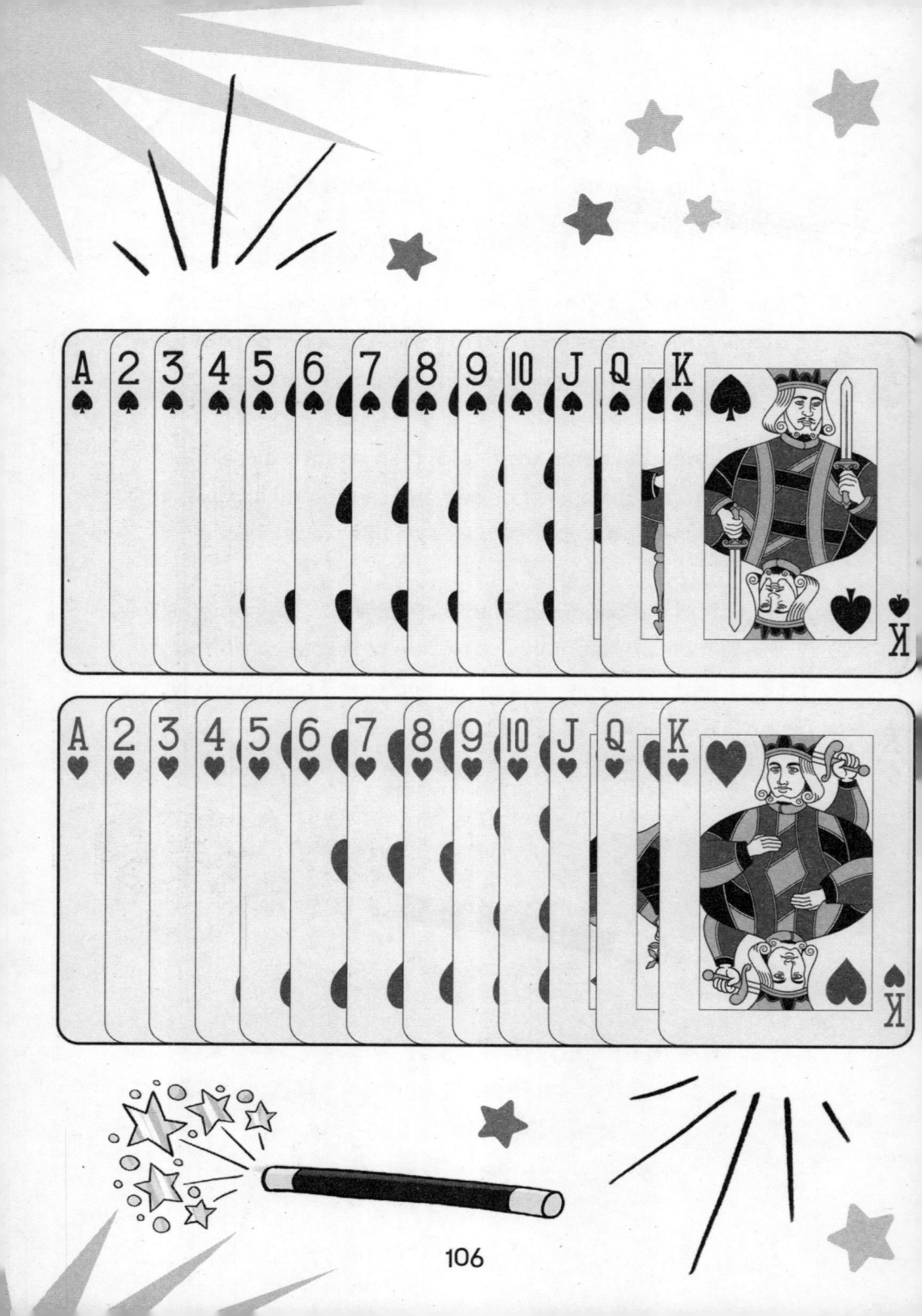

107

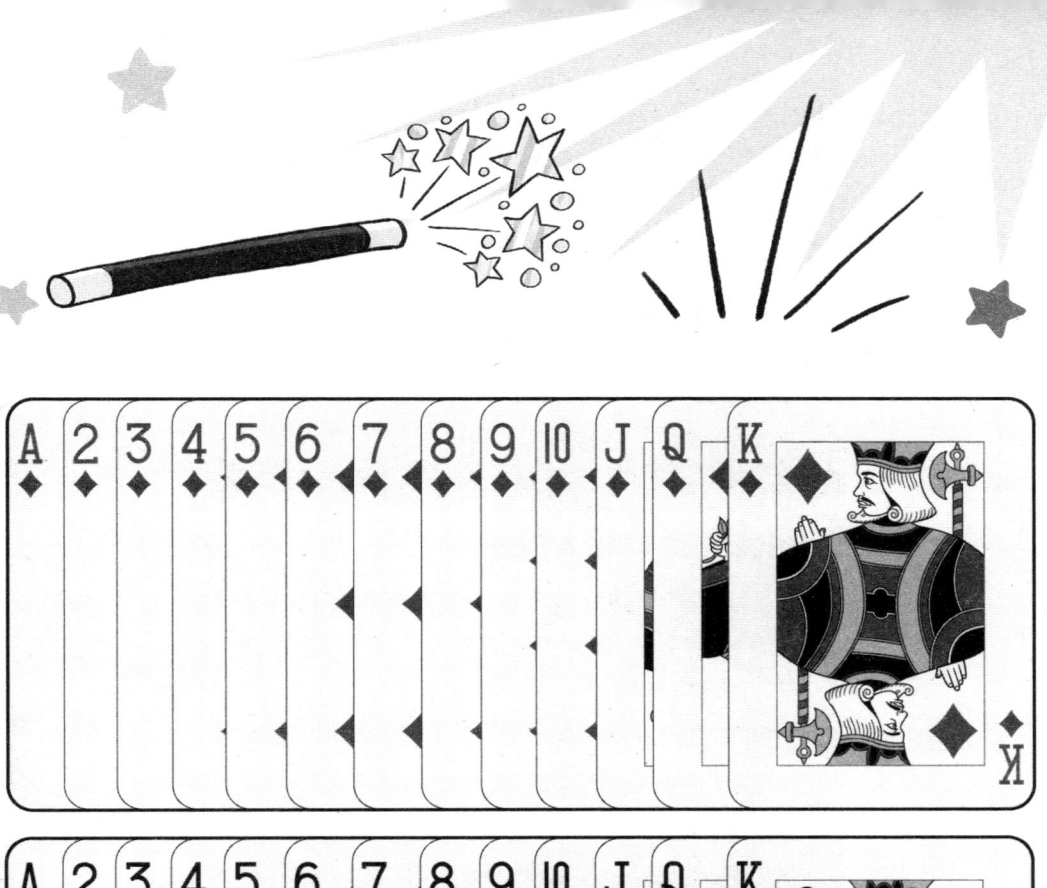

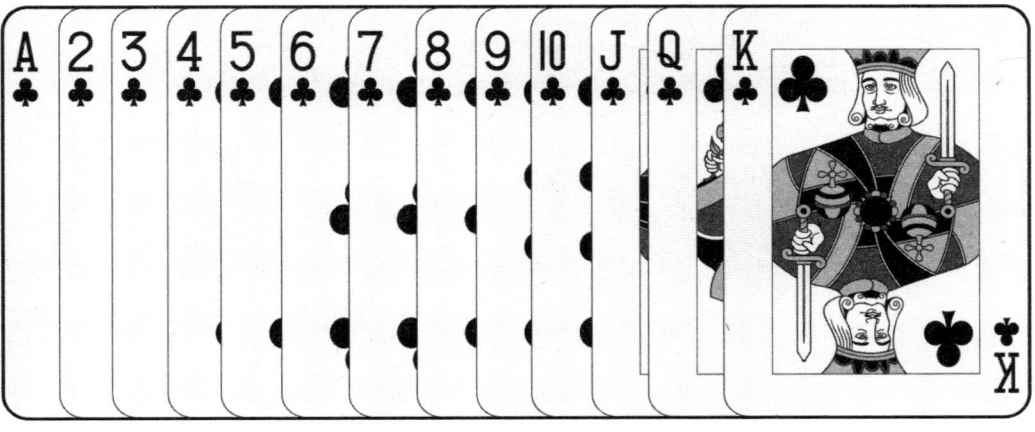

Hopefully, you will feel more confident about performing the card trick now, because you have thought about what might go wrong, taken steps to avoid the problems and have Plan B ready!

PROBLEM-SOLVING LIKE A PRO

These 'what if?' approaches can be applied to all the tricks that we have learned. Do you remember the one where you made a rubber band jump across your hand? What might go wrong and how can you try to avoid this happening? Well, maybe the rubber band decides to snap. This is more likely to happen with older bands, so you can try to avoid it by using a newer one. What will you do if the worst happens? One thing you can do is keep a couple of back-up rubber bands in your pocket. Then, if a band does snap, you can bring out another one and carry on with the trick.

You could also perform a different trick with the broken band . . .

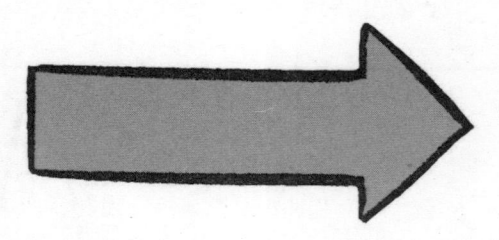

THE PERAMBULATING PAPERCLIP

Place a paperclip on to the broken band, about 5 cm from one end.

Place the rubber band into your left fist, making sure that the 5 cm section containing the paperclip sticks out at the top.

Now hold the band tightly between your left thumb and first finger.

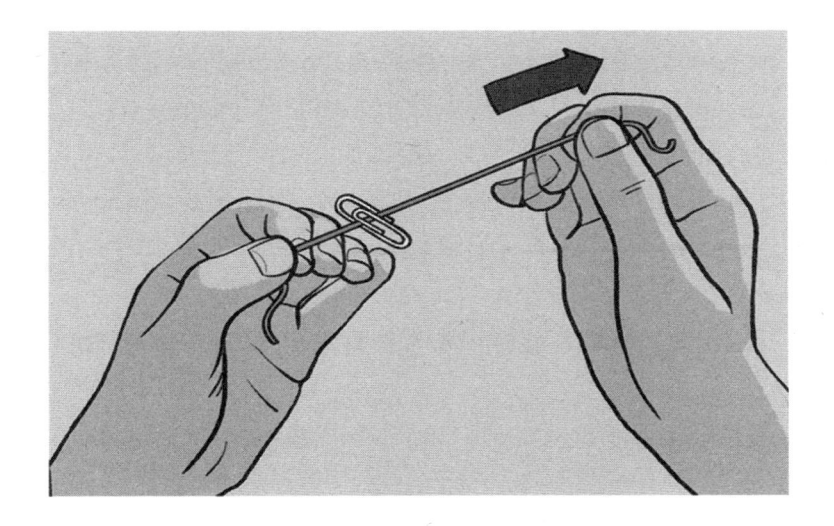

With your right hand, grasp the end of the band that is sticking out of your fist and carefully stretch it out.

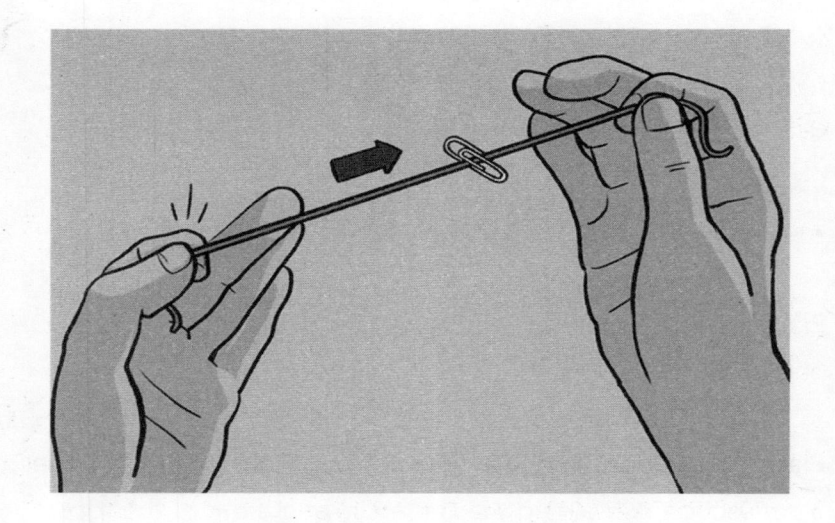

Gently release the pressure between your left thumb and finger and allow the band to slip out between them. As the band contracts, the paperclip will slowly move to the right. It looks as though the paperclip is magically creeping along the band! Like most good magic tricks, this one requires you to practice, but when you can perform the trick well it looks great.

Let's move on to the third stage of our magical guide to problem-solving . . .

3 KNOW WHAT TO DO WHEN IT ALL GOES WRONG!

From time to time, you will fall flat on your face (not literally!). Maybe your friend and everyone else in the group forgets the card, or they get confused and name the wrong card, or perhaps you don't have the piece of paper with 52 cards on it to hand. When that happens, here are a few ideas to help you.

- **Smile and laugh.** If you aren't too worried about things not going to plan, then your audience will be relaxed too. Here are some things to say that might make your friends laugh:

    'Ah, I forgot that this trick doesn't work on a Tuesday.'
    'Oh well, does anyone know any good jokes?'
    'Well, I wanted to surprise you with some magic, and instead, I have surprised myself.'

- **Learn from the setback.** What can you do to stop the problem happening in the future? Do you need a Plan C?

- **Don't worry.** When a trick hasn't worked out, performers often think that audiences will really remember it. In fact, most people aren't bothered and quickly forget.

- **Go easy on yourself.** None of us are perfect and even the greatest magicians mess up from time to time. If the trick was easy, it probably wouldn't fool anyone.

- **Look on the bright side.** If you are open about what has gone wrong, people are often quite supportive, and so it helps to bring out the best in them. We warm to people who are honest about their failings, and these setbacks can help you to bond with your friends and family.

THINK ABOUT WHAT YOU CAN DO (not what you can't)

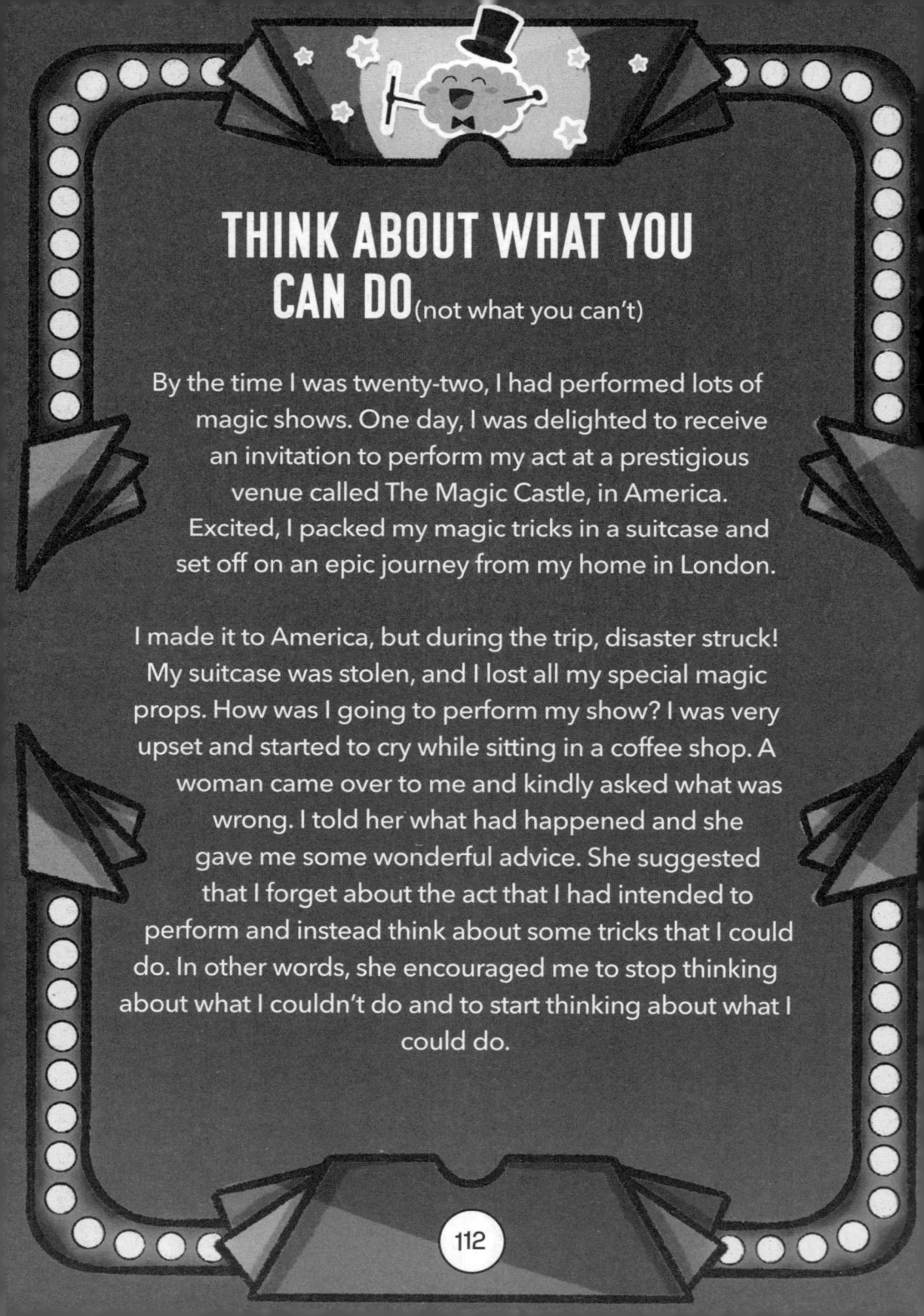

By the time I was twenty-two, I had performed lots of magic shows. One day, I was delighted to receive an invitation to perform my act at a prestigious venue called The Magic Castle, in America. Excited, I packed my magic tricks in a suitcase and set off on an epic journey from my home in London.

I made it to America, but during the trip, disaster struck! My suitcase was stolen, and I lost all my special magic props. How was I going to perform my show? I was very upset and started to cry while sitting in a coffee shop. A woman came over to me and kindly asked what was wrong. I told her what had happened and she gave me some wonderful advice. She suggested that I forget about the act that I had intended to perform and instead think about some tricks that I could do. In other words, she encouraged me to stop thinking about what I couldn't do and to start thinking about what I could do.

Straight away, I began to think about other tricks I could perform, including a great trick with a rubber band and some card tricks. I quickly worked on a new act. I thanked the woman, left the coffee shop and found the items for my new act. I spent the day rehearsing the new material and performed at The Magic Castle that night. All went well and I managed to snatch victory from the jaws of defeat!

The moral of the story is: when things go wrong, it's easy to give up. But focus on what you can do, rather than what you can't, and see if you can find a solution with what you have already.

These same ideas can be helpful in everyday life. It would be lovely if everything worked out well, but all of us trip up from time to time. It's good to be able to cope with these setbacks. Psychologists refer to this as **being resilient** and your new magical skills can help you to be prepared, to **bounce back and to keep going**. Let's imagine that you need to give an important talk, take an exam, go on a long journey or host a party.

Whatever the situation:

- It's good to be prepared.
- Think about what might go wrong and how can you try to avoid this happening.
- There is no need to imagine every possible problem, but it's good to think about the issues that are likely to crop up.
- Have a Plan B – if the worst happens, what are you going to do?
- Finally, when everything really goes wrong, use it as an opportunity to learn and don't be too hard on yourself . . . See if it helps you to become closer to those around you and remember that success often starts with setbacks.

IT'S NOT THE NUMBER OF TIMES THAT YOU FALL OVER THAT MATTERS; IT'S THE NUMBER OF TIMES THAT YOU GET UP AGAIN. BE RESILIENT!

SUPERPOWER 6

GROW YOUR CURIOSITY

Curiosity helps you to **grow your imagination**. Magicians love to find out how things work, and you can use your curiosity to explore the world and to expand your mind.

Let's start by travelling back in time . . .

Phew! It's now 1850, and we have arrived in a small but beautiful theatre in France. We are sitting in the audience and our fellow audience members are smartly dressed. The lights dim and the plush red curtains open to reveal master illusionist Jean-Eugène Robert-Houdin. The audience applaud as he takes a bow.

Robert-Houdin begins by showing his audience a small wooden box containing some money and explains that he has created a magical way of preventing the cash from being stolen. He needs a member of the audience to help him out and he chooses you!

The magician places the box on the stage and invites you to pick it up. You lift the small box with ease, as it's very light.

Robert-Houdin takes the box from you and sets it down on the stage again, while explaining to the audience that if a thief were to try to steal the box, he would use his magical powers to make it too heavy to lift. Robert-Houdin commands the box to be heavy and again asks you to lift it, but try as you might, you can't pick up the box! It's amazing, and the audience clap and cheer as you return to your seat.

It would be great to stay for the rest of the show but, alas, it's time for us to go back to the present.

Robert-Houdin was a remarkable man. When he first started to perform, he was very nervous, and his magic tricks often went wrong. However, he learned from his mistakes, kept going and eventually became famous throughout France as a great magician. Nowadays, he is often called 'the father of modern magic'. Before him, magicians tended to wear long robes and looked like wizards. Robert-Houdin performed in a smart evening suit and made magic much more fashionable.

He was fascinated by science and technology, and would use the latest discoveries to make his shows extra special. The light-and-heavy box is one of his most amazing inventions and, at the end of this chapter, we will discover its high-tech secret. First, let's delve into the curious world of science, mathematics and magic.

A PUFF OF AIR

Just like Robert-Houdin, magicians will often use the laws of physics to create their tricks. Let me show you what I mean. A puff of air tends to travel along surfaces. If you blow at the side of a drink can, the puff of air will cling to the sides of the can, curve around it and emerge on the other side. This is called the Coandă effect. Magicians have used this surprising scientific principle for centuries to make it look as if they can move objects with the power of their mind!

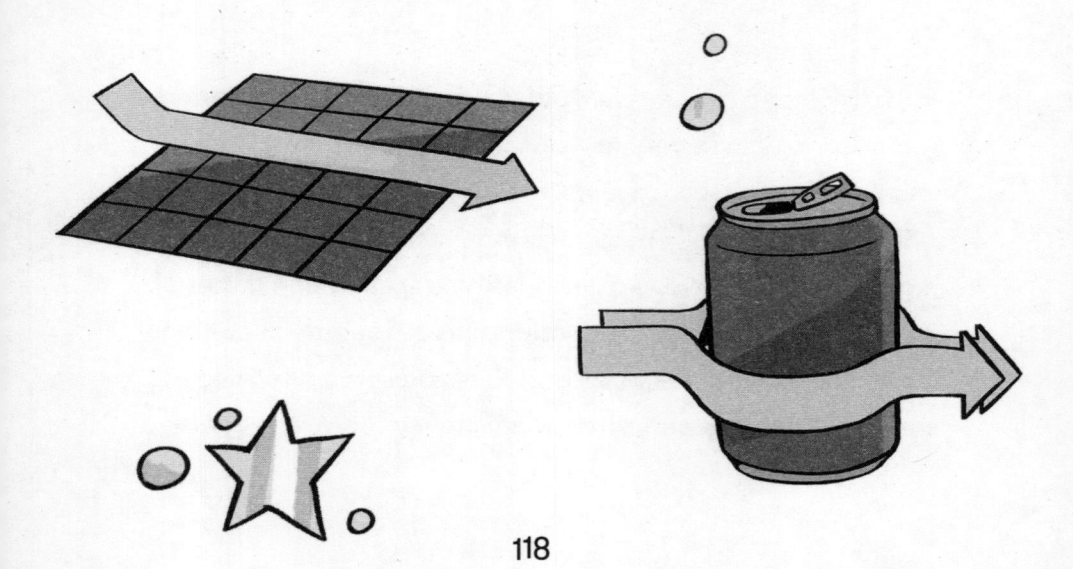

THE SENSATIONAL STRAW

Place a drinking straw on a table. Hold one hand a few inches above the straw and look down at it. Rub your thumb and fingers together and, at the same time, secretly blow towards the table. The puff of air will hit the table, travel along it and make the straw roll away from you. People won't notice you blowing, because they will be focusing on the straw, so it will look like the act of rubbing your thumb and fingers together made the straw move!

You could even rub your hand on your sleeve before holding it above the straw. That way, it will look like you are using static electricity to make the straw move.

THE MYSTERY OF THE RED CARDS

Like lots of magicians, I am very curious and love thinking about how I can use science and technology to make magic. A few years ago, I came across a high-tech model toy car. The car was cleverly designed and used optical sensors to follow a black line drawn on a piece of paper. I played around with the toy and came up with a magic trick for my YouTube channel.

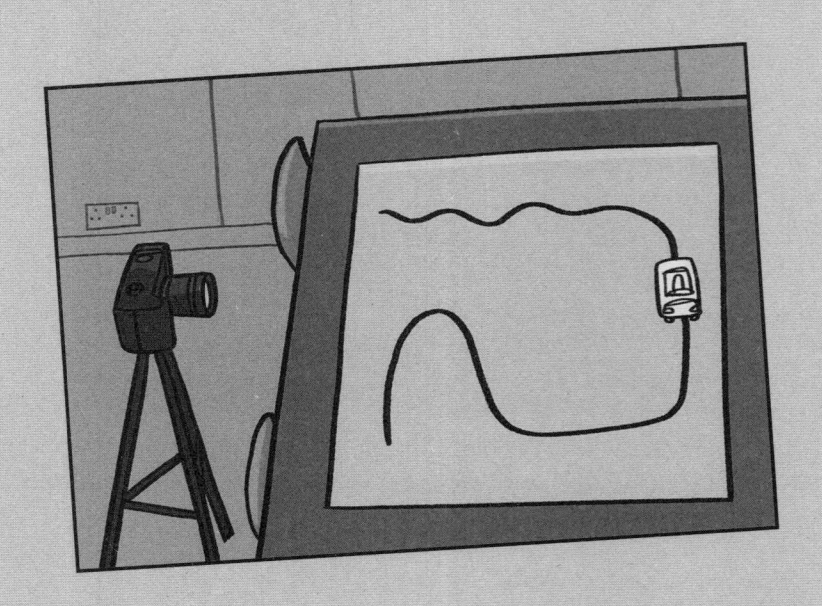

I drew a long and wiggly line on a big sheet of paper, placed the car on one end of it and put two small red cardboard screens in front. Then I turned the car on, and it began to trundle along the line. As it drove around, I moved the screens, making sure that they were always in front of the car. To viewers, it looked as if I were just moving the screens around – they had no idea that the car was hidden behind them. Because the car followed the line, I knew exactly where it was heading and so could use the screens to cover it up.

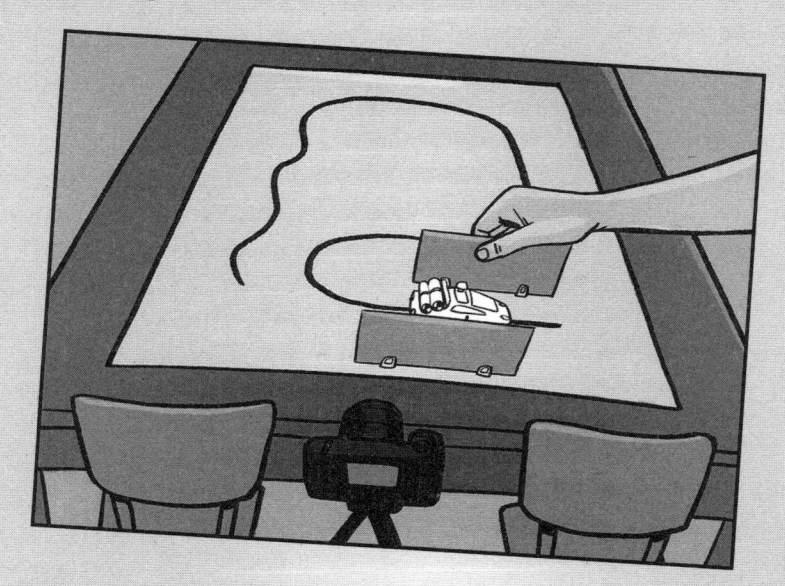

At the end of the video, I moved the screens apart and suddenly the car appeared. The video is called 'The Mystery of the Red Cards' and it attracted several million views from around the world. You can watch it on my Quirkology YouTube channel.

MATTER THROUGH MATTER

Let's learn another science-based magic trick. You will need a piece of paper about the size of a banknote and two paperclips.

Imagine that the paper has two lines drawn on it, like this:

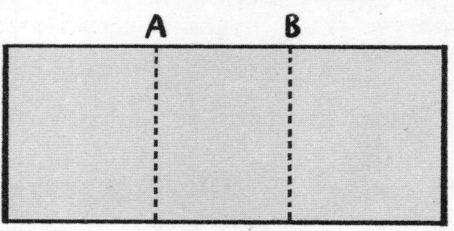

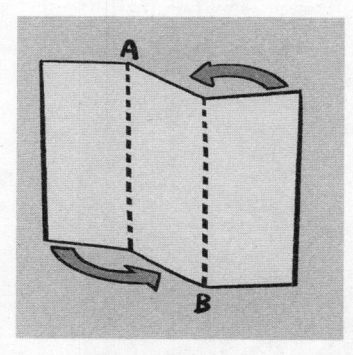

Fold the left edge towards you along Line A, and then fold the right edge away from you along Line B.

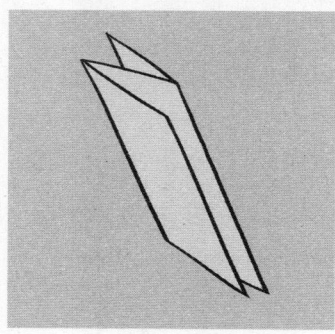

Seen from above, the folded piece of paper will now look like the letter Z.

Next, clip one of the paperclips to the back two folds of the paper close to Line A, and the other paperclip to the front two folds of the paper close to Line B.

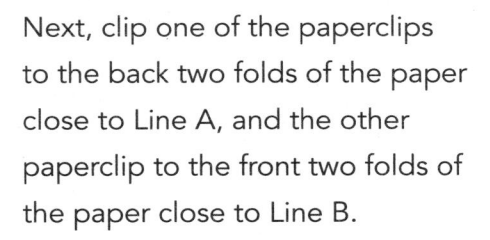

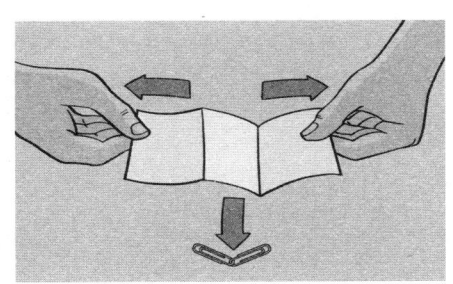

Hold on to the left edge of the paper in your left hand and the right edge in your right hand. Now you are ready for the big moment. Slant the top of the paper (containing the paperclips) away from you and quickly pull the two edges apart to straighten the paper back out.* The two paperclips will jump into the air and magically link together! You might have to do this a few times to get the hang of it, but after that you will be able to do it every time.

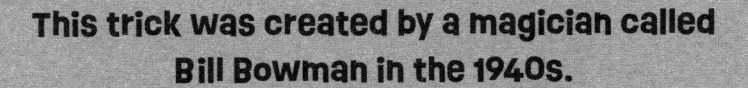

This trick was created by a magician called Bill Bowman in the 1940s.

There are lots of ways of presenting the trick. Maybe you could say that the two paperclips are good friends and like spending time together. Or explain that you are certain you can make the two paperclips land on the table and touch one another. I once showed the trick to a rocket scientist and he created a lovely

*Beware of flying paperclips! Remember, safety first! Always slant the paper away from you and your friends.

presentation in which one paperclip represented a spacecraft leaving the Moon and the other represented a spacecraft going around the Moon. The paperclips linking together showed how the two spacecraft joined together before coming back to Earth.

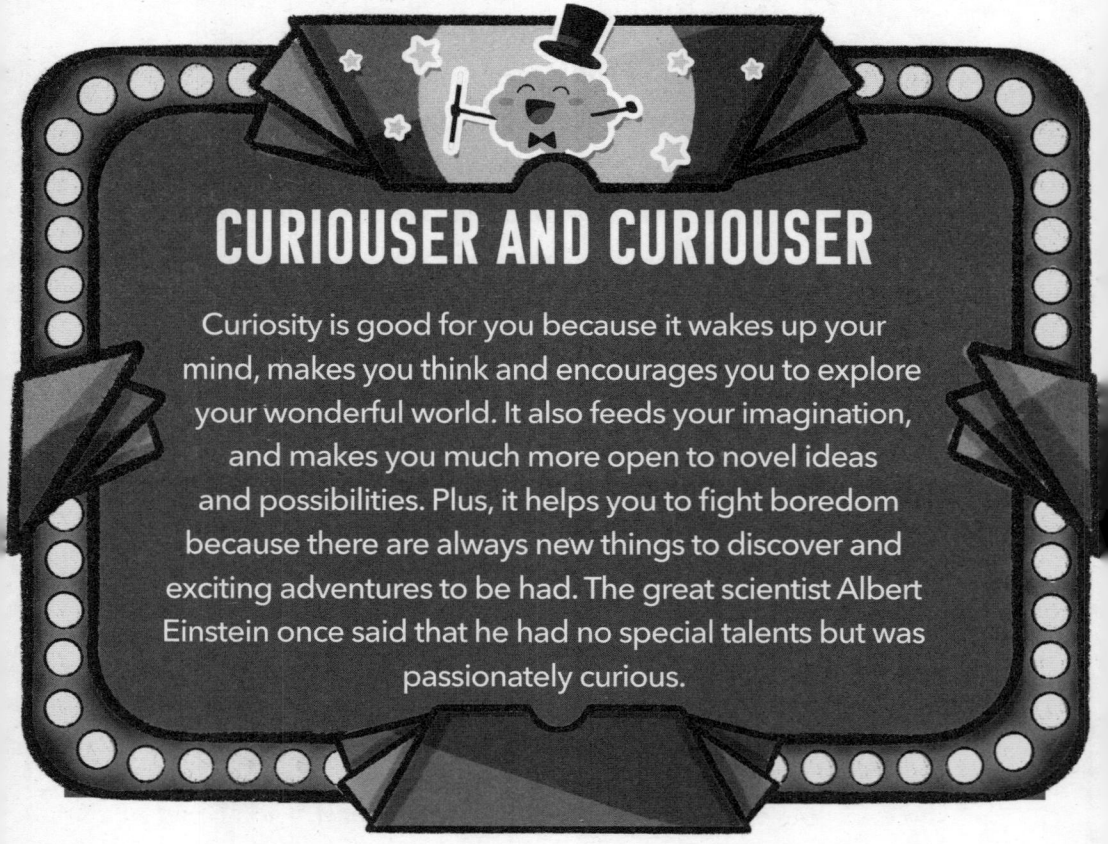

CURIOUSER AND CURIOUSER

Curiosity is good for you because it wakes up your mind, makes you think and encourages you to explore your wonderful world. It also feeds your imagination, and makes you much more open to novel ideas and possibilities. Plus, it helps you to fight boredom because there are always new things to discover and exciting adventures to be had. The great scientist Albert Einstein once said that he had no special talents but was passionately curious.

To become curious, it's good to experiment and explore by asking: 'What happens when . . .?' Let's try it now.

What happens when you hang a thin rubber band over Line A and put a paperclip on the two front layers of the paper, close to Line B? The paperclip will link to the rubber band. What happens when you put a rubber band over Line A, one paperclip on the back two layers of the paper close to Line A, and the other paperclip on the front two layers of the paper close to Line B? Amazingly, the two paperclips link on to the band!

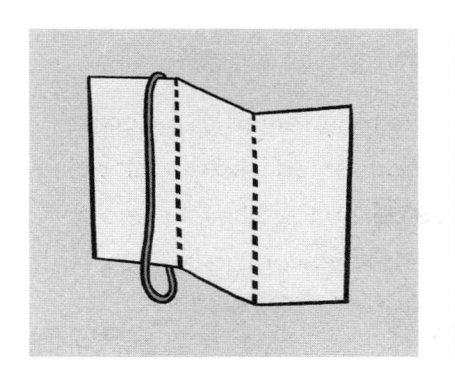

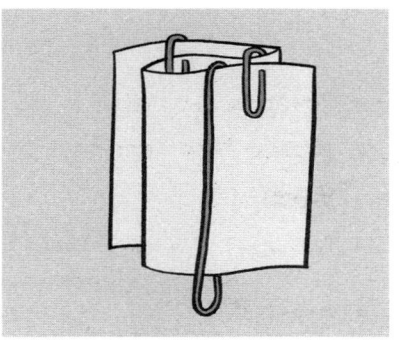

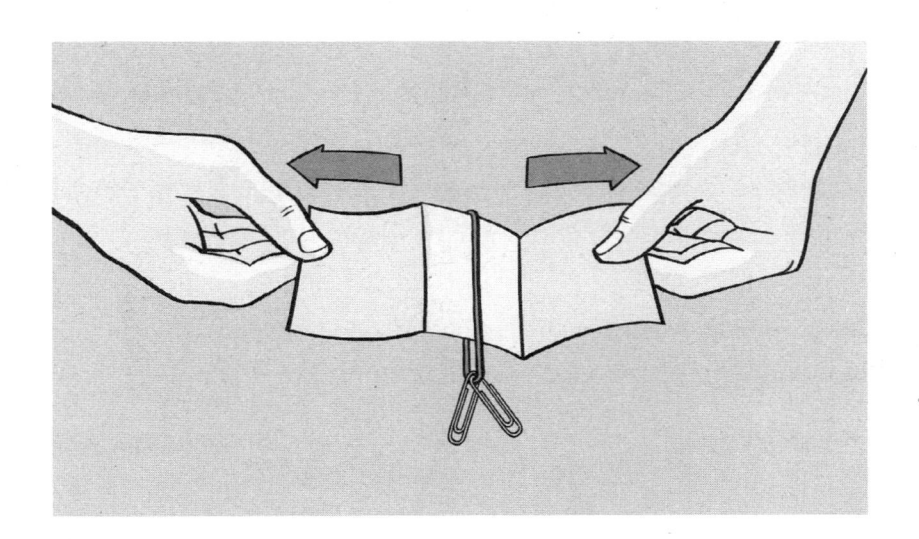

We have used the magic of science to make a straw roll across a table and to link two paperclips together. Now let's get curious about some mathematical mysteries.

MATHS MAGIC

Lots of mathematicians love magic, and they have discovered some jaw-dropping facts and figures about playing cards. For instance, how many ways can you arrange all 52 playing cards in the deck? The answer is that there are about . . .

80,000,000,000,000,000,000,000,000,000,000,000, 000,000,000,000,000,000,000,000,000,000 combinations.

That's more than the number of stars in our galaxy and the grains of sand on Earth. That means that when you shuffle a deck, the cards have probably never been in that order before in the entire history of the Universe and will never be in that order again!

Magicians and mathematicians have also created some wonderful number-based tricks. Let's perform one now.

THINK OF A NUMBER

We are about to discover your lucky animal. Please think of the date on which you were born. So, if you were born on 7 May, you would think of the number 7 and if you were born on 18 October, you would think of the number 18. With that number in mind, please carry out the following instructions. Feel free to use a calculator.

> **Double your number.**
> **Add 10.**
> **Divide the total by 2.**
> **Finally, subtract the number that you started with.**

You now have a new number in your head. My first prediction is that this new number is between 1 and 10. Am I right? Great. Now look at the following list and find your lucky animal:

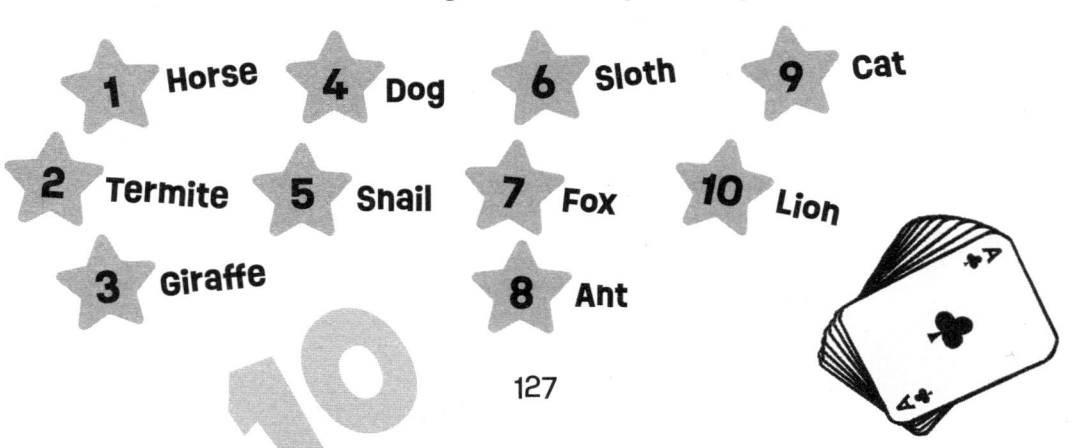

1. Horse
2. Termite
3. Giraffe
4. Dog
5. Snail
6. Sloth
7. Fox
8. Ant
9. Cat
10. Lion

Focus on your animal. I am receiving your thoughts. The image is coming through very slowly. Ah, I am not surprised, because you are thinking of a SNAIL!

Let's discover the mathematics behind this lovely illusion.

$$Y=t\{56x276.67\}/q+32.98 - 9f6.7xd$$

I'm joking. Let's explore, experiment and ask:
'What happens when . . .?'

What happens when we start with the number 2? Doubling it makes 4, adding 10 makes 14, halving that makes 7, and subtracting the first number (2) leaves 5.

What happens when we start with the number 25? Doubling it makes 50, adding 10 makes 60, halving that makes 30, and subtracting the first number (25) leaves 5.

Try some other numbers and see what happens. You will always end up with the number 5 and the snail!

As ever, there are lots of ways of presenting this trick. Rather than asking your friend to use their birthdate, you could ask them to think of any number. And instead of pretending to read your friend's mind, you could predict their lucky animal by drawing a picture of a snail on a piece of paper.

There is, however, a slight problem. If you show the trick to several people, they might talk about it and discover that they all ended up with the snail. We can solve this problem by getting even more curious and digging deeper into the mechanics of the trick.

The second line of the instructions says . . . **Add 10.**

What happens when we change the number 10 to the number 6? The instructions are now:

> **Double your number.**
> **Add 6.**
> **Divide the total by 2.**
> **Finally, subtract the number that you started with.**

What happens when we start with the number 2? Doubling it makes 4, adding 6 makes 10, halving that makes 5, and subtracting the first number (2) leaves 3.

What happens when we start with the number 25? Doubling it makes 50, adding 6 makes 56, halving that makes 28, and subtracting the first number (25) leaves 3.

Try replacing the number 6 in the second line of the instructions with other EVEN numbers and see what happens. The final number is always half of the number on the second line of the instructions. That's good because you can now change that number each time you repeat the trick and have your friends end up with different animals. Problem solved!

THE MAGIC CIRCLES

This next piece of maths magic involves the illustration on the next page. As you can see, it contains lots of drawings of animals. Please choose one by following these instructions.

Think of a number between 5 and 20.

Put your finger on the X.

Count out your chosen number by moving one space at a time. Follow the footsteps, and then move into and around the grey circles.

When you have finished counting, keep your finger where it is, and then count out your number again, but this time moving the opposite way around the grey circles.

The circle you land on shows your chosen animal.

Now focus on your chosen animal. Is it the SNAIL again? This is a fun trick that you can show your friends.

Hopefully, you are feeling curious, wondering how it works. Can you figure it out by asking: 'What happens when . . .?' For instance, what happens when you choose different numbers? What happens when you change the drawing so that there are two footsteps? What happens when you change it so that there are more animals in the circle?

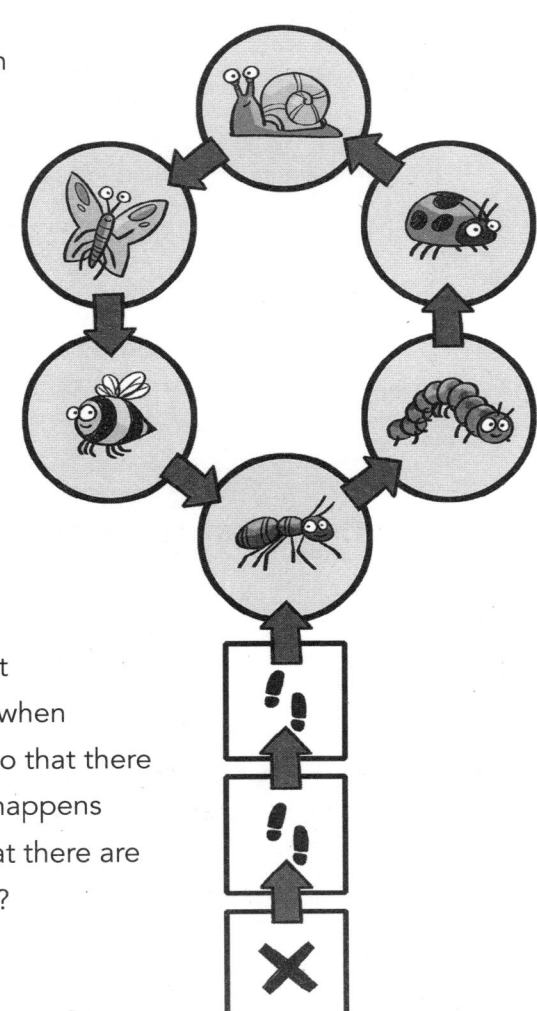

131

THE HUMAN CALCULATOR

Tell your friends that you can think faster than a calculator! Ask them to think of any three-figure number. Let's imagine that they choose 453. Next, ask them to use a calculator to multiply their chosen number by 7, then multiply the result by 11 and then multiply that result by 13. While they are doing this, you quickly write down:

453,453.

Your friends carry out the following calculations . . .

453 x 7 = 3,171
3,171 x 11 = 34,881
34,881 x 13 = 453,453

. . . and discover that your instant calculation was correct! How does it work?

Well, 7 x 11 x 13 = 1,001, and any three-figure number multiplied by 1,001 is a repetition of itself. If your friends choose 285, you write 285,285. If they choose 837, you write 837,837. To appear to be a human calculator, write down their number twice.

It's good to be curious in everyday life. Here are three tips that will help you to stay curious:

- **Feed your mind.** Be curious about anything and everything that interests you. Go to museums and art galleries. Search the internet for the latest amazing technology. Read books and listen to podcasts. Look out for mysteries and puzzles. Your world is a wonderful place, and you can use interesting information and stories to entertain other people and to make them curious too.

- **Ask 'why?'.** When you see something that you don't understand, try to find out what's going on. Remember that there is no such thing as a silly question.

   Here are a few questions to get you started. Why do people say 'cheese' when they have their photograph taken? Why are danger signals on roads often red? Why can you raed tihs snetnece eevn thuogh the letrets are in the wnorg oderr?*

*Saying 'cheese' forces your face into a smile, the colour red has a long wavelength and so is easier to see from a distance, and your brain predicts what the words should be, as long as the first and last letters aren't altered.

- **Explore.** Scientists, magicians and other curious people love to roll up their sleeves and carry out experiments. Feel free to play around and to explore. Build something and discover what happens when you change it. Ask: 'What happens when . . .?' Find out by doing.

Talking of curiosity, have you been thinking about Robert-Houdin and his mysterious box? The box that was light one moment and heavy the next? To make the trick work, he used a remarkable piece of technology called an electromagnet. Unlike regular magnets, electromagnets only work when they have electricity running through them. Today we use electromagnets to lock doors, slow down trains, play music through headphones and much more, but in Robert-Houdin's time, most people didn't know about electromagnetism. The magician hid an electromagnet under the stage and attached a small sheet of iron to the bottom of the box. When the electromagnet was turned off, the box could easily be picked up. However, when the electromagnet was turned on, the box became stuck to the stage and so felt as if it had suddenly become very heavy! What a clever and curious magician!

Be curious.

Feed your mind with interesting ideas.

Ask 'why?' and 'what happens when . . .?'

Play, investigate and explore.

SUPERPOWER 7

IMPROVE FOCUS AND BOOST YOUR BRAIN POWER

Being able to focus and concentrate your brain power is important in everyday life because it means that you can **learn and remember things, plan, make better decisions, achieve your goals** and much more. Magicians are great at focusing because they must learn new tricks, practise actions again and again, and concentrate when they are performing. Let's find out how you can use magic to gain these important skills.

Before we start, I would like to introduce you to a friend of mine called Laura London. Laura is a very successful magician, and she performs all over the world. When she was a child, she often rushed from one thing to another, didn't sleep very well, had difficulty controlling her behaviour and struggled to focus on any one topic.

Eventually, Laura's teachers said that she was unlikely to do well in school or to get a job. Laura's mother encouraged her to learn a musical instrument, which helped Laura a bit. However, the real difference came when Laura discovered magic.

When she was eight years old, Laura saw a magician perform and became fascinated by the art of conjuring. She eventually went to a magic shop and bought some tricks. She really enjoyed practising those and started to find out more about magic. After learning several tricks, Laura discovered that she especially liked manipulating playing cards because it involved lots of repetition. Repeating the same actions again and again was relaxing, and it helped to improve her focus and self-control. Also, magic was fun, and it gave her a way of entertaining her friends.

Laura eventually became the youngest-ever female member of The Magic Circle and started working as a magician. She is now great at manipulating cards, has a wonderful act and gives talks about how **magic can help people to boost their self-control, focus and concentration**.

Here's some magic that requires your full attention . . .

HAND TO HAND

We will start with the type of playing-card manipulations that fascinated Laura when she was young.

> **Some playing cards are plastic-coated and others are linen-coated. When you are manipulating cards, try to use the linen-coated ones because they glide over one another, whereas the plastic-coated ones tend to stick together.**

Let's learn how to spread the cards from hand to hand . . .

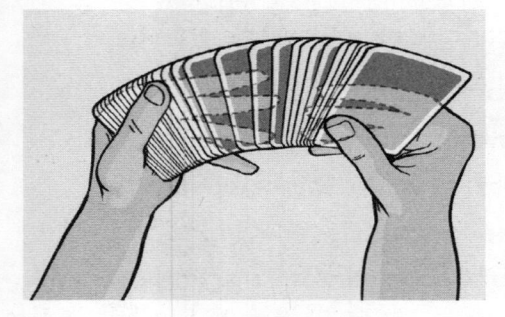

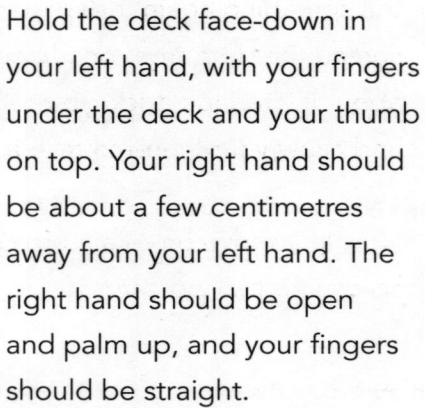

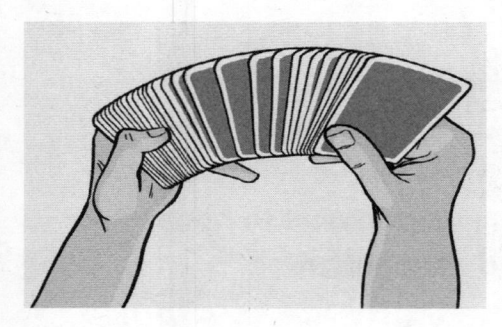

Hold the deck face-down in your left hand, with your fingers under the deck and your thumb on top. Your right hand should be about a few centimetres away from your left hand. The right hand should be open and palm up, and your fingers should be straight.

Now use your left thumb to push off some of the top cards over to the right. The cards are pushed between your right-hand fingers and thumb, and your right hand supports the cards as they move across.

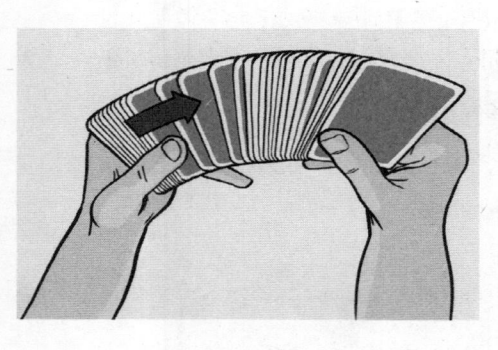

Continue to use your left thumb to push more and more cards into your right hand.

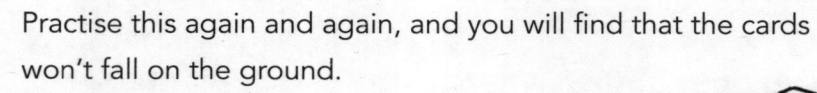

Practise this again and again, and you will find that the cards won't fall on the ground.

Once you get towards the end of the deck, place the cards in your right hand back into your left hand and then repeat the spreading again. Keep practising and you will be able to spread the deck from one hand to the other without thinking about it. During a trick, you can perform the spread slowly and allow your friend to take a card.

Now let's move on to a more challenging way of spreading playing cards.

THE RIBBON SPREAD

This is a very impressive manipulation that involves spreading a deck of cards across a table, like a ribbon. Ideally, the table should be covered with a tablecloth.

Hold the deck palm-down in your right hand, with your thumb pressing against the short edge of the deck closest to you, your second and third fingers against the short edge of the deck furthest away from you, and your first finger resting on the left long edge of the deck.

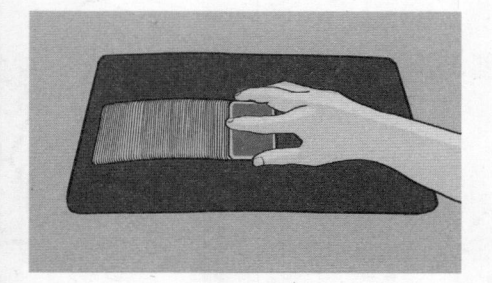

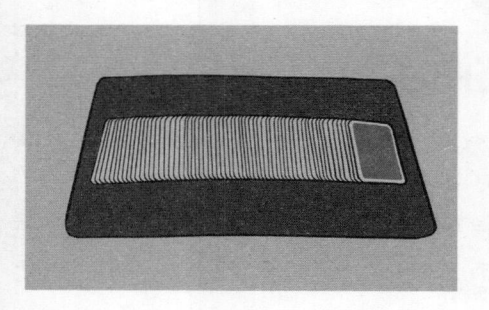

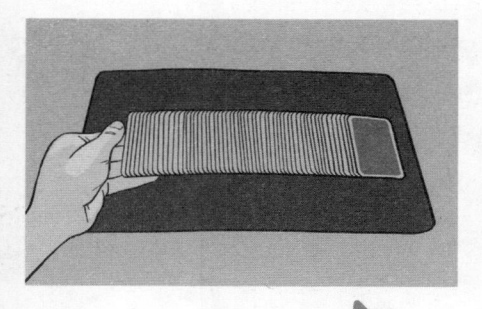

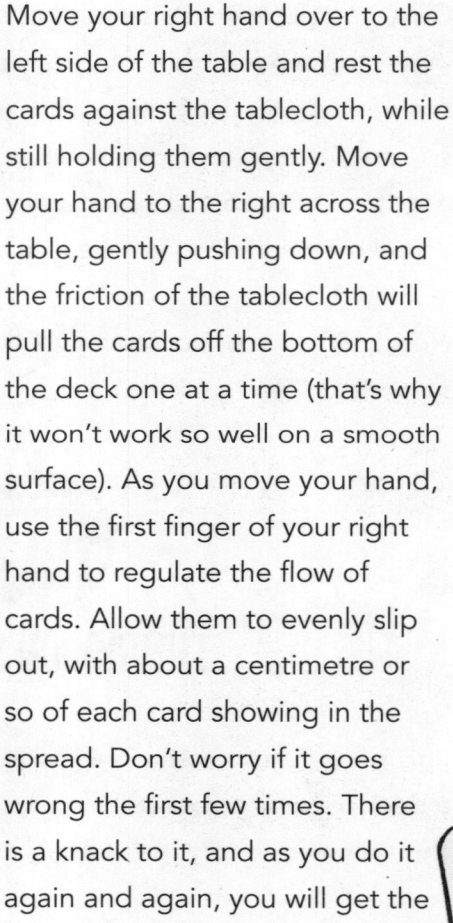

Move your right hand over to the left side of the table and rest the cards against the tablecloth, while still holding them gently. Move your hand to the right across the table, gently pushing down, and the friction of the tablecloth will pull the cards off the bottom of the deck one at a time (that's why it won't work so well on a smooth surface). As you move your hand, use the first finger of your right hand to regulate the flow of cards. Allow them to evenly slip out, with about a centimetre or so of each card showing in the spread. Don't worry if it goes wrong the first few times. There is a knack to it, and as you do it again and again, you will get the idea.

Once you have mastered the move, you can learn how to pick up the cards. Hold your left hand palm-up and place your first, second and third fingers under the card on the far left of the spread, with your thumb hovering above the spread. Now move your hand to the right and scoop up the cards. Some magicians do a variation of this: they take the top card from the right-hand side of the spread, place it under the bottom card on the left-hand side of the spread and then use it to scoop up the deck.

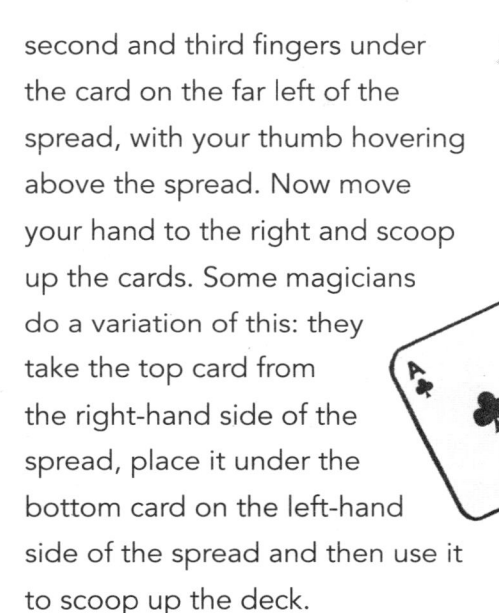

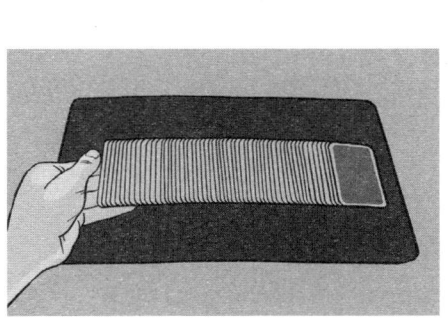

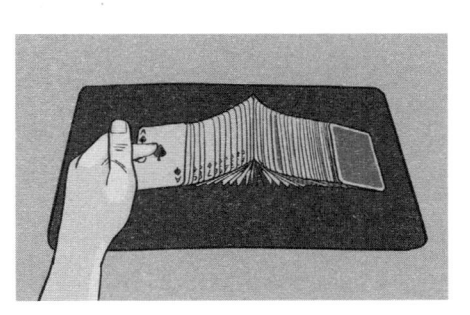

Once you are comfortable with the spread and scoop, you can try turning the spread over. This time you will definitely need a table or flat surface covered with a cloth because this move just won't work on a smooth surface. After you have made a spread, turn your left hand palm-up, and place your first, second and third fingers under the bottom card on the left side of the spread. Now gently flip the bottom card over to the right, keeping its right edge touching the table. The other cards will flip over one by one like dominos, which looks great. As before, some magicians find it helpful to take the top card from the right-hand side of the spread, place it under the bottom card on the left side, and then use it to turn over the spread.

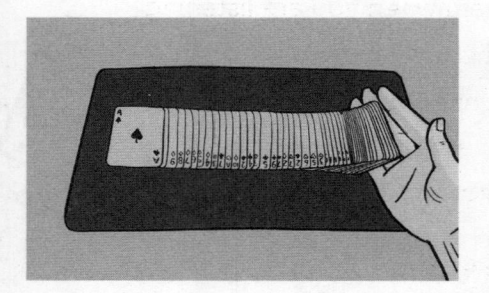

Once the cards have flipped over, you can hold your right hand palm-up, put your fingers under the card on the far right-hand side of the spread and do the same thing but in the opposite direction. This will make the cards flip over in the opposite way.

You can even try to make part of the spread stand up, then take a single card and run it back and forth along the top edges of the spread!

These moves are not easy, but you will be able to perform them if you keep on repeating them. Make sure that you can do each step before moving on to the next and give yourself time off when the going gets tough. Remember to always learn from your mistakes. You might find it helpful to practise at the same time each day, and to remind yourself that even a small amount of progress is still progress.

Once magicians have mastered the moves, they often find it relaxing to carry out the manipulations again and again, because it takes their attention away from other distractions and concerns. You can even do them when you are listening to your favourite music.

When you have learned these moves, you can use them to perform one of Laura London's favourite illusions.

THE TWISTER

Before you begin, place the Joker on the bottom of the deck. If you don't have the Joker, you can use any other card, as long as you can remember it.

Start by spreading the cards face-down from hand to hand and asking your friend to take one. Once your friend has chosen, push the rest of the cards back together and reassemble the deck. Ask your friend to look at their chosen card. Turn away while they do this so that you don't see the card.

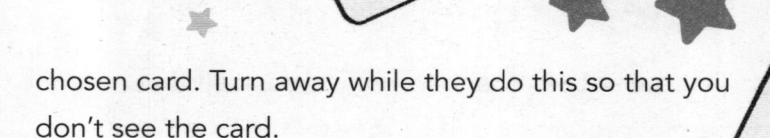

When you turn away, secretly do two things. First, turn the deck over so that it is face-up in your hands. Hold the deck in your left hand, with your fingers on one long side and your thumb on the other long side. The Joker will be face-up on top. Second, turn the Joker face-down.

Turn around and face your friend. The deck looks the same, but every card below the top card is face-up. Take your friend's card in your right hand and carefully push it face-down anywhere into the middle of the deck. You can do this by pushing it into the narrow end of the deck that is closest to your friend. Be careful not to show that all the cards, except for the Joker, are face-up.

Place the deck behind your back and say that you need the help of your favourite card, the Joker. Slide the top card (the Joker) from your left to right hand, bring out the Joker and say something like, *'Ah, here is my favourite card, that was lucky!'*. Place the Joker on the table. Now bring out the deck and place it face-down on the table. Say that you will wave the Joker over the deck, and this will cause your friend's card to turn face-up! Ask your friend to tell you their card and then ribbon-spread the deck on the table. If you don't have a big enough table, spread the cards from hand to hand. Either way, your friend will be amazed to find that their card really is facing the opposite direction to all the others!

Now let's turn our attention to some tricks that are designed to really boost your concentration and focus.

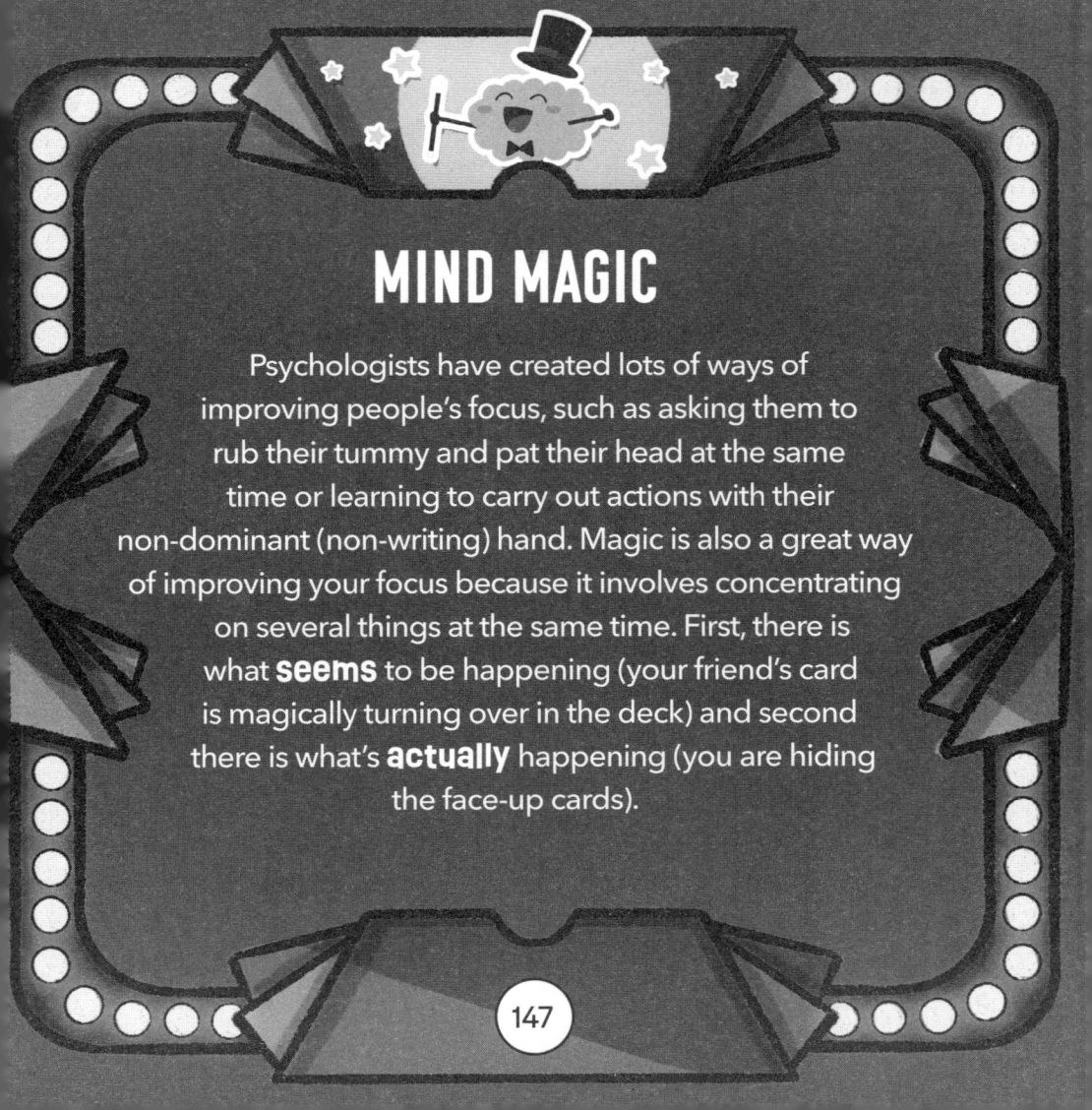

MIND MAGIC

Psychologists have created lots of ways of improving people's focus, such as asking them to rub their tummy and pat their head at the same time or learning to carry out actions with their non-dominant (non-writing) hand. Magic is also a great way of improving your focus because it involves concentrating on several things at the same time. First, there is what **seems** to be happening (your friend's card is magically turning over in the deck) and second there is what's **actually** happening (you are hiding the face-up cards).

SPELL-O-MATIC

For this illusion, you need 13 playing cards that run Ace to Ten, then a Jack, a Queen and a King. It's nice if the cards are all the same suit (such as diamonds or clubs), but it's fine if they are from different suits. Arrange the cards in this order:

THREE, EIGHT, SEVEN, ACE, QUEEN, SIX, FOUR, TWO, JACK, KING, TEN, NINE, FIVE

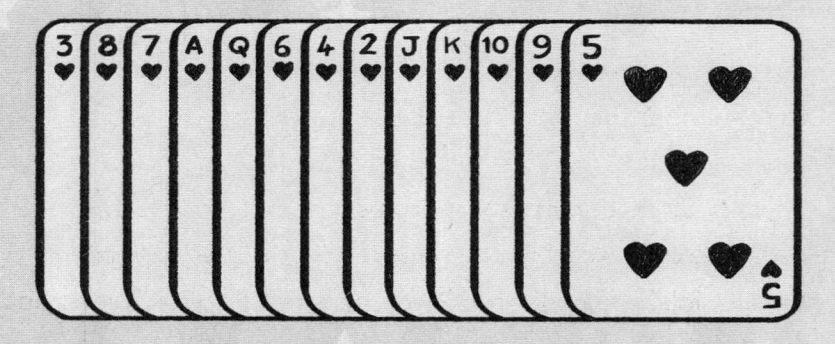

Hold the 13 cards face-down. The Three should be on top and the Five should be on the bottom. Now spell the word ACE out loud and move a card from the top to the bottom of the stack as you say each letter. So as you say A, take off the top card and place it on the bottom, then say C while taking the new top card and placing it on the bottom, and then finally say E and take the new top card and place it on the bottom.

148

Turn over the new top card and it will be the Ace. Place the Ace face-up on the table. Now carry out the same movements as you spell the word TWO. As you say T, take the top card and put it on the bottom. And the same for W and then again for O. Now turn over the new top card and it will be the Two!

Place the Two face-up on the table and repeat the process for the word THREE, and then for FOUR, and then for FIVE, and so on for all the numbers. Eventually, you will spell out JACK, QUEEN and KING. Each time, you will find that the correct card appears on the top, even when you only have two cards left to count.

To really develop your focus and concentration, you could try to remember the initial order of the cards.

There is another great version of this trick that requires a complete deck. Arrange the cards so that the four Aces are on the top, followed by the four Twos, and then the four Threes, and so on through to the four Kings. To perform the trick, start by spelling the word ACE, moving a card from the top to the bottom of the deck as you say the letters A and C, and then turning the new top card face-up as you say the letter E. It's an Ace!

Place the Ace face-up on the table. Now repeat the same actions for the word TWO — again, turning the top card face-up as you say the letter O. And, again, place the Two on the table.

Work your way through all the other values (Three, Four, Five, Six, Seven, Eight, Nine, Ten, Jack, Queen and King) and you will find that the correct card appears each time.

You will end up with 13 face-up cards on the table. Now deal the top three cards face-down on to the Ace, the next three cards face-down on to the Two, and so on through the deck. When you turn these cards face-up, you will see that now all the Aces have found one another, and the same with the Twos and the Threes, and so on. It looks amazing!

This wonderful trick encourages focus and planning, and was invented by a magician called Ralph Hull.

MY STORY

Magic really helps me to concentrate. When I was a child, I really struggled to read and so didn't spend very much time looking at books. Then I became fascinated by magic, and wanted to read about the amazing exploits of master magicians and their mind-blowing illusions. This motivated me to focus, and I started to enjoy other types of books too.

Magic also helps me to plan. Once I had learned some good tricks, I started to perform magic at children's birthday parties. This was helpful because I had to create a list of the tricks for the show, make sure that I had all the apparatus that I needed, arrive in plenty of time and ensure that my performance wasn't too short or too long.

There was also my little blue book. After each performance, I wrote down the tricks that I had used so that if the same person wanted another show, I could arrive with new ones. Having said that, over forty years later, I still haven't had anyone ask me to perform a second time. Just joking! I still have that little blue book and it's a lasting reminder of how magic helped me to plan ahead and to be reliable.

THE CHOICE IS YOURS

This illusion requires you to concentrate *and* to think on your feet. It is performed with any five items. All the items need to be too large to be hidden in your hand, and could be borrowed from your friends and family. Let's imagine that you have . . .

PHONE   **PEN**   **TOY**
   COMB   **PENCIL**

Write the name of any one of the items on a piece of paper, fold it up so your friend can't see what is written on it and place the paper on the table. Let's imagine that you have written the word PENCIL. This is your prediction, and you are going to carry out a series of actions that will ensure that it's always correct.

Magicians refer to this as a 'force' because it feels like a free choice, but the item that you predicted will always be chosen. It is called the **P.A.T.E.O. (Pick Any Two, Eliminate One) Force**, and it was created and popularised by two British magicians called Roy Baker and Ken de Courcy. It's good for your mind because it requires you to remember how it works and to concentrate during the performance.

Place the items into a paper or cloth bag. Explain that both you and your friend are going to take it in turns to reach into the bag and randomly pick up any two items, and then your friend will choose which one of them is to be discarded.

You start. Reach into the bag and pick up one item in your right hand and another in your left hand. Ask your friend which one you should discard. It doesn't matter which items you pick up, as long as you do not go for your predicted item, in this case, the PENCIL. Let's imagine that you pick up the COMB and the PHONE, and your friend asks you to discard the COMB. Put the COMB to one side and the PHONE back in the bag. You will be left with . . .

PHONE   **PEN**   **PENCIL**   **TOY**

Ask your friend to reach into the bag and to randomly pick up any two items. If they do not pick up the PENCIL, then it doesn't matter which item you ask them to discard. However, if they pick up the PENCIL, then ask them to discard the other item. Let's imagine that they pick up the PENCIL and the TOY, and you ask them to discard the TOY. They put the PENCIL back in the bag and you will be left with . . .

PHONE   **PEN**   **PENCIL**

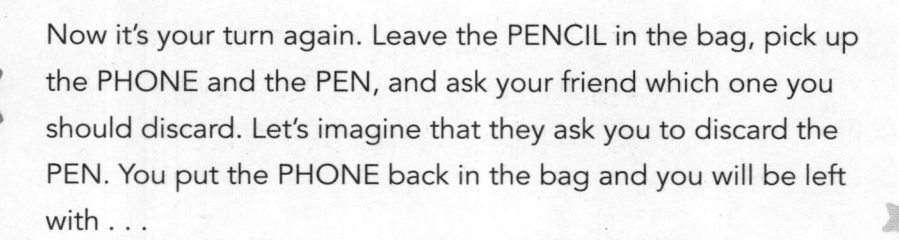

Now it's your turn again. Leave the PENCIL in the bag, pick up the PHONE and the PEN, and ask your friend which one you should discard. Let's imagine that they ask you to discard the PEN. You put the PHONE back in the bag and you will be left with . . .

PHONE   **PENCIL**

Now your friend picks up the two remaining items and you ask them to discard the PHONE. That leaves them with the PENCIL, and when they open the piece of paper, they will see that your prediction is correct!

In short, you never pick up the item that you have predicted, and if your friend picks it up, you discard the other item.

You can also perform the trick with playing cards. It is much more impressive if the cards are face-down. To do this, place a small pencil dot on the back of your predicted card – something you can spot but isn't obvious to people who don't know it is there – and then avoid picking up that card yourself or discard it if your friend chooses it.

Being able to focus your mind is important in everyday life because it helps you to:

**Plan ahead.
Remember important information.
Make better decisions.**

Magic is a great way of improving your focus because it encourages you to study instructions, practise lots and remember what to do during a performance. Try these tricks and moves, and see if they bring out the magic in your mind.

Discover the magic of being able to focus your brain power!

Pay attention.

Practise.

Plan ahead.

SUPERPOWER 8

CONJURE UP CREATIVITY

We have already discovered how learning magic gives you **seven superpowers**. Now it's time to unlock the **eighth**, and perhaps the most important one of all: **CREATIVITY!**

Your imagination is **amazing**. It allows you to **generate new ideas**, to **think about exciting things** that might happen in the future, to **express your feelings and thoughts in creative ways** and to be **original**. Magic boosts your imagination because it involves coming up with new ways to present magic tricks, as well as creating and decorating apparatus. Let's use the **power of magic** to boost your creativity.

Here's a great card trick to get your creative juices flowing!

CRISS-CROSS CARD MAGIC

Before you begin, draw the Three-and-a-Half of Clubs (yes, you heard that right!) on a piece of paper . . . like this. It doesn't matter if your drawing isn't very good (mine isn't!). Just try your best and have fun.

Place your drawing face-down on a table. You will also need a deck of cards. Place the Seven of Clubs face-down on the top of the deck and put the deck face-down on the table.

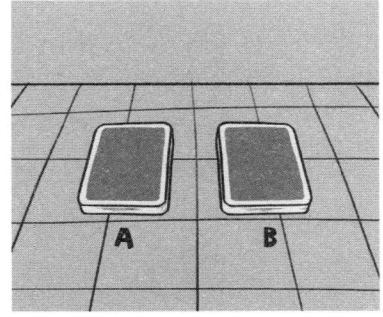

To perform the illusion, ask your friend to lift off as many, or as few, cards as they want from the deck. Let's call the cards in their hand Group A and the cards remaining on the table Group B.

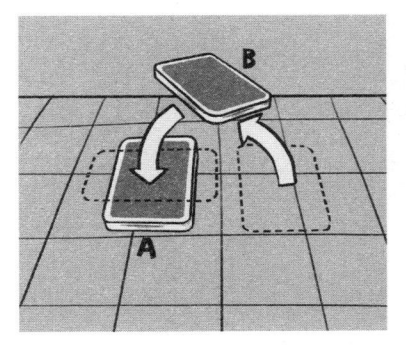

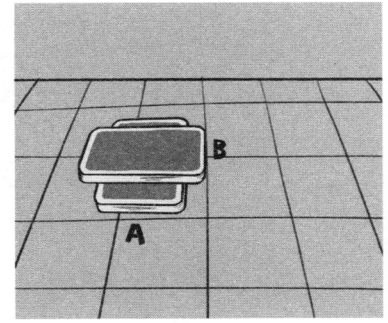

The Seven of Clubs will be on top of Group A. Ask your friend to place Group A face-down on the table and then casually say something like, *'Great. Let's mark the cut.'* Lift Group B, turn it 90 degrees and place it on top of Group A to form a cross.

Now we need to add a little bit of time so that your friend doesn't become suspicious about what's going on. You could say something like, *'My prediction has been on the table all this time and I cannot change it.'* Or you could build up the drama by saying something like, *'This trick sometimes doesn't work, so don't get too excited!'*

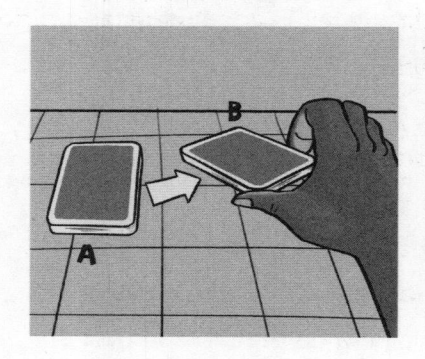

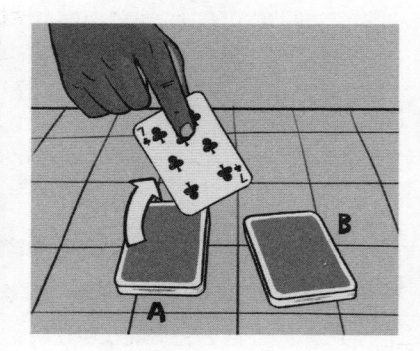

Then pick up Group B, point to the top card of Group A and say, *'Can you please look at your card, and make sure that I don't see it?'* Your friend will pick up the card that is on top of Group A.

It looks like a free choice because they could have divided the deck anywhere, but they have been made to choose the Seven

This great trick was invented by an American magician called Max Holden almost a hundred years ago.

of Clubs. If you find it hard to see how it works then turn the Seven face-up and follow the actions. You will see that they will always end up with that card.

Now ask your friend to halve the number on their card, and to name the number and suit that they are thinking of. They will say the Three-and-a-Half of Clubs. You then turn over the paper and show that your prediction is correct!

Let's use our creativity to think of other ways of presenting the trick. Here are a few ideas.

Draw the Seven of Clubs on a piece of paper, fold it up and put it in your shoe. Then write 'Please look in my shoe' on another piece of paper and place that face-down on the table. After your friend has chosen the Seven of Clubs, turn over the paper on the table and look surprised. Then take off your shoe and show that it contains the correct card!

Write 'Magician predicts the Seven of Clubs' in large letters on a sheet of paper and stick it to the front of a newspaper so that it looks like a dramatic headline. Fold up the pages, perform the trick and then unfold the newspaper to reveal your prediction.

Draw a Nine of Clubs on a piece of card but tear off the bottom two clubs. Put the card in your pocket or bag. After your friend has looked at their card, reach into your pocket or bag and slowly start to take out the Nine of Clubs. Your friend will think that your prediction is wrong, but then they will see that two of the clubs are missing and that you have correctly predicted the Seven of Clubs.

WHAT ELSE COULD YOU DO?

There is no perfect answer. Just make up something that suits you and that is fun for your friend. Maybe you will create something that no one has ever thought of before!

THE SCIENCE BIT

Two other psychologists and I recently conducted a scientific experiment into magic and creativity. The study involved a group of schoolchildren who were around ten years old. We arranged for these children to carry out a creativity test that involved them coming up with different uses for everyday objects, such as a paperclip, a piece of paper or a magazine.

We gave each child a creativity score by counting how many uses they came up with. Then some of the children were shown how to perform a magic trick and the others were given an art lesson. After they had finished performing magic and creating art, the children took the creativity test again. We found that the children who had learned magic obtained much higher scores than those who had been given the art lesson. Maybe everyone should be taught magic in school!

THE BAFFLING BOOMERANGS

Now let's make some more magic apparatus. Carefully trace the two boomerang shapes shown below on a piece of paper, or photocopy this page, and then cut out the shapes (but make sure you copy the sizes exactly!).

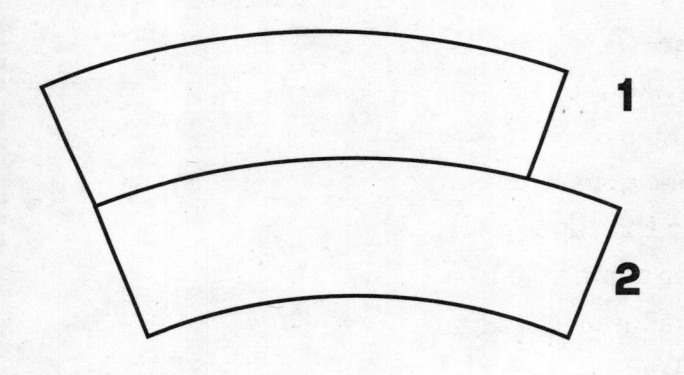

Place one boomerang above the other. Which one seems larger? Now swap them around. Which one seems larger now? You will discover that **the top boomerang always appears smaller than the bottom one**. But if you place one boomerang directly on top of the other, you will see that they are the same size. When you show your friends the trick, you could just point out that the top shape always looks smaller than the bottom shape. However, it's possible to make the trick more interesting by decorating the boomerangs and telling a fun story. For instance, you could draw a green banana on one boomerang and a yellow banana on the other, and then say:

The other day I was very hungry, and I found these two bananas in the cupboard. The green one was on the top shelf and the yellow one was on the bottom shelf.
(Put the green banana boomerang above the yellow banana boomerang.)

It was clear that the yellow banana was bigger, but just as I reached into the cupboard, I sneezed and, suddenly, the two bananas changed places!
(Put the yellow banana boomerang above the green banana boomerang.)

Now the green banana was larger than the yellow one! Then everything became really confusing because I took both bananas out of the cupboard and they were the same size.
(Put the two boomerangs on top of one another.)

It drove me bananas!

This trick probably won't fool your friends. However, the tale of the two bananas might make them smile and it's a great way of developing your **storytelling skills**. Let's explore a few other ways of presenting the trick.

This curious optical illusion was made popular by a German psychologist called Franz Carl Müller-Lyer more than a hundred years ago.

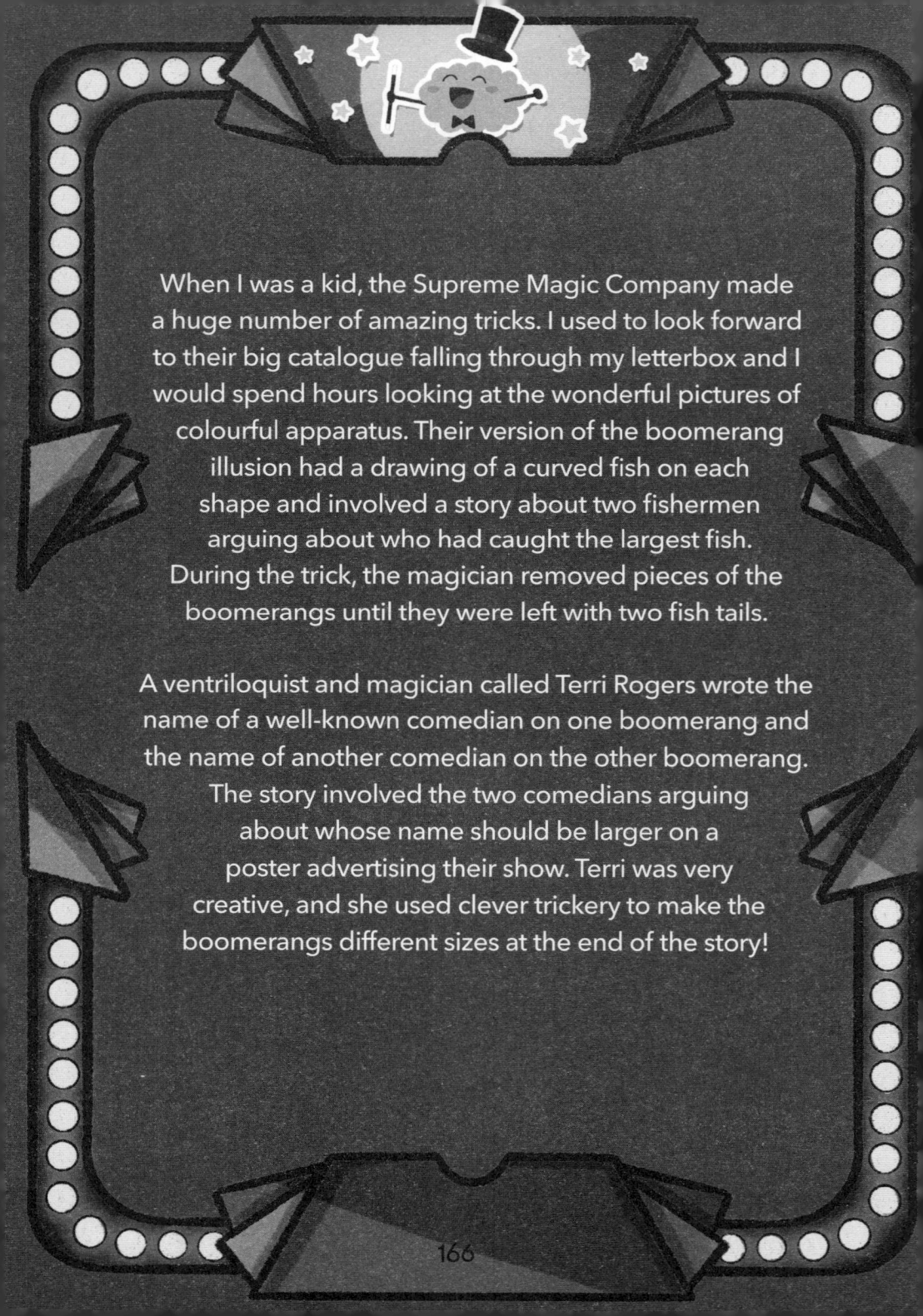

When I was a kid, the Supreme Magic Company made a huge number of amazing tricks. I used to look forward to their big catalogue falling through my letterbox and I would spend hours looking at the wonderful pictures of colourful apparatus. Their version of the boomerang illusion had a drawing of a curved fish on each shape and involved a story about two fishermen arguing about who had caught the largest fish. During the trick, the magician removed pieces of the boomerangs until they were left with two fish tails.

A ventriloquist and magician called Terri Rogers wrote the name of a well-known comedian on one boomerang and the name of another comedian on the other boomerang. The story involved the two comedians arguing about whose name should be larger on a poster advertising their show. Terri was very creative, and she used clever trickery to make the boomerangs different sizes at the end of the story!

Recently, another creative magician called David Regal made a version that used four boomerangs. Two of the boomerangs were yellow and had the word 'short' printed on them, and the other two boomerangs were red and had the word 'long' printed on them. David tells a fun story about architects becoming confused as they try to use the blocks to design a building.

One of my favourite presentations was created by a Scottish magician called Ian Adair. He drew a caterpillar on each boomerang. When the two boomerangs were turned over and brought together, they created a picture of a beautiful butterfly.

TELLER'S MAGIC!

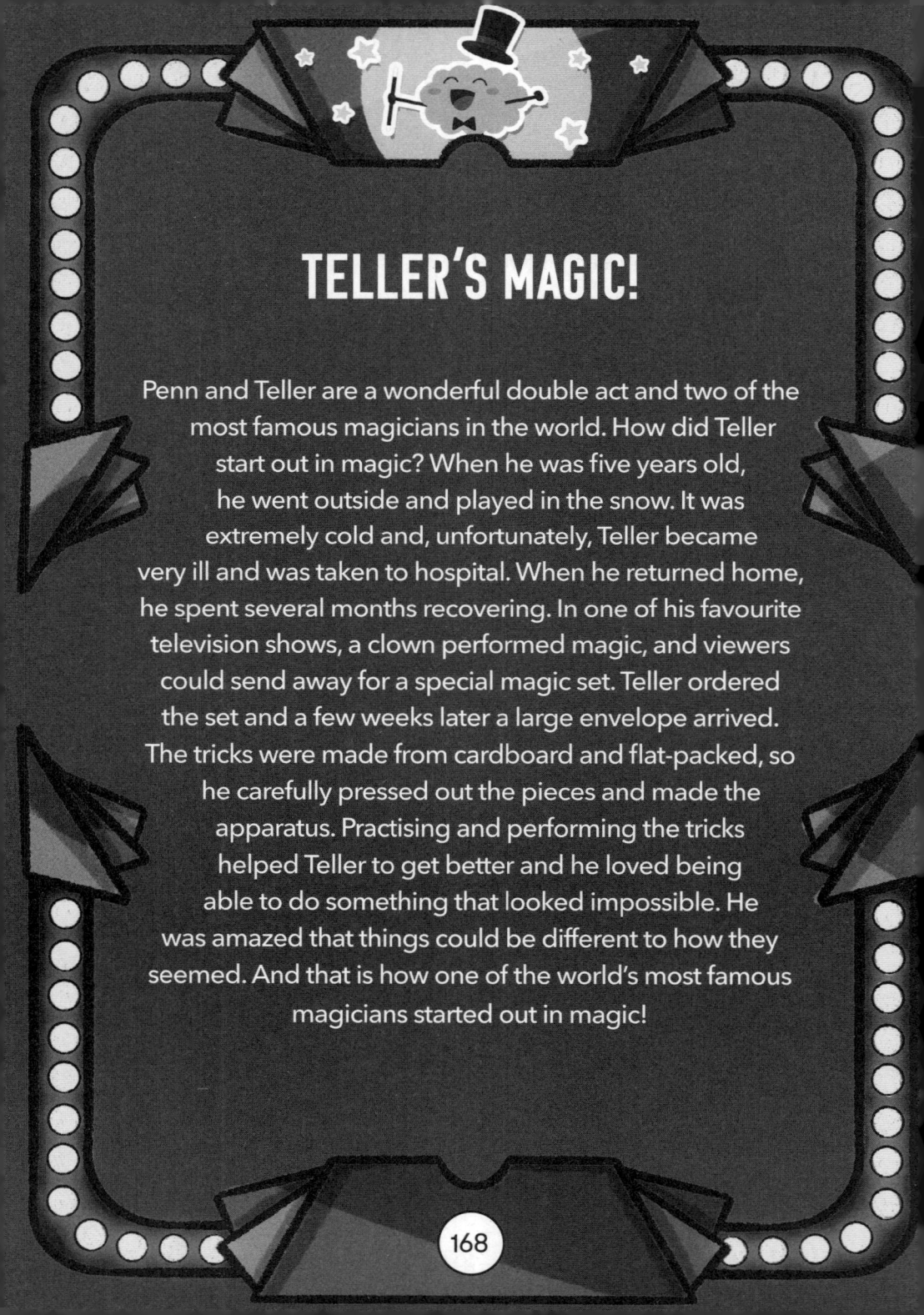

Penn and Teller are a wonderful double act and two of the most famous magicians in the world. How did Teller start out in magic? When he was five years old, he went outside and played in the snow. It was extremely cold and, unfortunately, Teller became very ill and was taken to hospital. When he returned home, he spent several months recovering. In one of his favourite television shows, a clown performed magic, and viewers could send away for a special magic set. Teller ordered the set and a few weeks later a large envelope arrived. The tricks were made from cardboard and flat-packed, so he carefully pressed out the pieces and made the apparatus. Practising and performing the tricks helped Teller to get better and he loved being able to do something that looked impossible. He was amazed that things could be different to how they seemed. And that is how one of the world's most famous magicians started out in magic!

How could you decorate your boomerangs? How about drawing a picture of yourself on one and your friend on the other? Or making each boomerang look like a sock? Or drawing a rainbow on each of them? What story could you tell? Are you and your friend arguing about who is the tallest? Are you trying to find socks that fit? Did you see two rainbows and try to figure out which one was the biggest? Could you pretend to use the power of your mind to convince your friend that one of the boomerangs is bigger than the other? Or use them to demonstrate a new type of paper that grows and shrinks? Also, don't forget that there are two sides to the boomerangs. Play, explore, create and find something that suits you and your personality.

THE BOOK OF MAGIC

So far, we have been creating apparatus by drawing on pieces of paper. Now let's move on to something more challenging. Magicians enjoy creating apparatus out of paper, cardboard, wood, cloth, plastic or anything else that comes to hand. One of my favourite performers is Mario the Maker Magician, whose show is full of homemade apparatus that he has constructed from cardboard, tin cans and sticky tape. He even found out how to write computer programs so that he could create homemade electronic robots that perform magic. Mario's show is based around three simple but wonderful ideas: **do what you love, use what you have and have fun.**

Let's develop your maker skills and transform an ordinary notebook into an extraordinary illusion!

In this trick, you flick through a notebook and show that the pages are blank. Then you blow on it and suddenly it becomes **full of magical pictures**.

You will need a notebook that has about 20 to 30 pages and a soft cover and back so that you can easily flick through it. The pages need to be quite thick, so that the drawings don't show through.

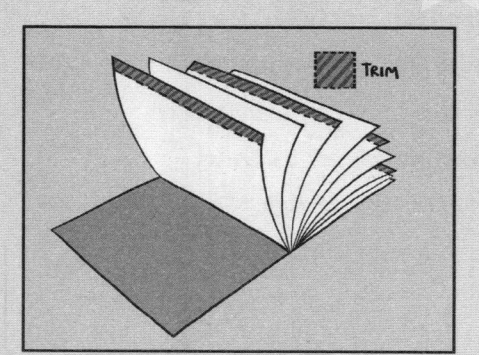

Open the notebook so that the inside of the cover is on your left and Page 1 is on your right. Use a pair of scissors to carefully trim about 5 mm off the long right-hand edge of the first page and every second page after that. You will end up with each page having one of two widths – and the pages alternating between narrow and wide, narrow and wide, and so on – throughout the notebook.

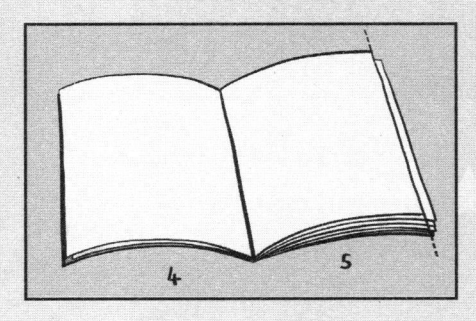

Turn over Page 1, so that you are now looking at Page 2 (on the left) and Page 3 (on the right). Cover both Page 2 and Page 3 in fun magical drawings, like top hats, wands, stars, question marks, dice and playing cards. Turn the page and leave Page 4 and Page 5 blank. Then turn the page again and add more magic drawings to Page 6 and Page 7. Turn the page and leave Page 8 and Page 9 blank. And so on through the book.

Remember, safety first! Be careful when you are using scissors and always ask an adult to help you.

To perform the trick, rest the spine of the notebook on your right hand and use your left hand to flick through the pages, going from the back to the front. Because of the wide and narrow pages, the notebook will seem blank. Blow on the book and then rest the spine on your left hand and use your right thumb to flick through again, but this time going from the front to the back. Now the pages will magically be full of wonderful drawings.

Maybe you can tell a little story:

This is my magical notebook. It is full of wonderful drawings but only magicians can see them. To most people they are invisible.
(Flick through the notebook, showing the blank pages.)

However, I can make you a magician for a few moments...

CLICK YOUR FINGERS!

...and now you will be able to see the drawings.
(Flick through the book again, showing that all the drawings have appeared.)

Unfortunately, when the magic wears off, the pages will look blank again.
(Flick through the notebook one last time, showing the blank pages.)

This illusion has a very long history. Do you remember Reginald Scot from the section 'Superpower 4: Master Magical Teamwork'? He wrote about magic in 1584 and described magicians using this kind of notebook all those years ago!

GET CREATIVE

This trick is great for **developing your creativity** because the notebook can be decorated in lots of ways and used to tell **many different stories**. You could fill it with drawings and tell your friend that it belonged to a famous artist who had a dream in which they made hundreds of sketches, and when they woke up, they found that their notebook was filled with illustrations. You could write on the pages and say that it is your **secret diary**, or you could put black and white drawings on the 'blank' pages and coloured drawings on the others, and make the drawings **magically colour themselves in**. Perhaps you could write equations in the book and say that it comes from scientists trying to discover **the secret of invisibility**, or draw maps on the pages and explain how it was **used by spies to conceal important information** from the enemy during a war. How will you decorate your notebook? **What story will you tell?**

When you create a story, it's good to think about what people will find interesting and entertaining. Maybe you can invent a story that is **funny**, **dramatic**, **surprising** or based around **something that happened to you?** Could it involve a dream that you had? Maybe a fairy tale that you have heard, a historic event or a scientific breakthrough? Perhaps it could encourage people to look after the planet or to be kind to one another? David Brookhouse is a magician, a teacher and a friend of mine. He encourages children to visit local museums and heritage sites, and to create magic to tell stories associated with the objects, buildings and people that they find there. Maybe you could try that? **Try to tell stories that suit you and your personality**.

THE COLLEGE OF MAGIC

The College of Magic is one of the most amazing places in the world. It is based in South Africa and for more than forty years it has taught magic to hundreds of young people. The College does a wonderful job of promoting creativity and celebrating South Africa's cultural diversity. I recently teamed up with the College and helped to write a book about the great work that they do. Some of their students are from communities that are often sidelined in society, and their experiences will shape how they see and perform magic. Like any performing art, magic grows and develops when people from different backgrounds are involved.

Time to create more amazing magical apparatus! You will need some boxes of different sizes . . .

THE MAGIC BOXES

I love making magic tricks out of cardboard. It's quick to do and if you make a mistake, you can throw it away and start again. In my office I have a big box filled with different types of cardboard boxes and tubes, and I use these to play and to experiment. A few years ago, I helped to create an **entire magic show out of cardboard boxes**, which was lots of fun and encouraged the audience to use their imagination. You can make the next trick out of cardboard boxes and, because it's larger than the previous tricks in this book, it's great to perform this to a group of people. It is known as **The Square Circle** and was invented by a magician called Louis Histed in the 1930s.

You show two empty boxes and can then produce lots of items from them. Let's imagine that you are going to make an orange appear.

You will need three cardboard boxes that fit inside one another. You can either find these around your house or make them yourself. Let's call them the **Large Box**, the **Medium Box** and the **Small Box**. The image on the next page shows the sizes of the boxes that I use.

Carefully cut off the top and the bottom of both the Large Box and the Medium Box, so that you are left with just the four sides. Now cut off the top of the Small Box. Next, stick black velvet all around the **inside** of the Large Box, and all around the **outside** of the Small Box. You can buy sticky-backed velvet from craft shops or online. Finally, carefully cut out a diamond shape into one wall of the Large Box. In my Large Box, this is about 10 cm high and 10 cm wide.

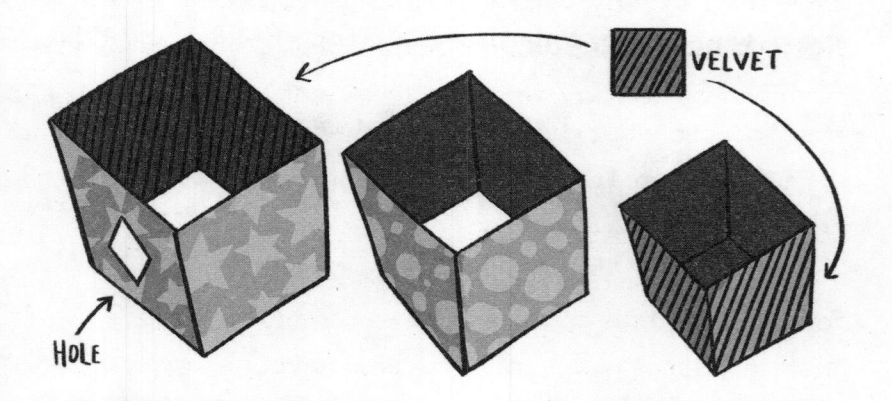

VELVET

HOLE

Remember, safety first! Be careful when you are using scissors and always ask an adult to help you.

Next, **place an orange inside the Small Box**. Then place the Small Box on a table, put the Medium Box over it and finally place the Large Box over the Medium Box.

Here's how to perform the trick: pick up the Large Box and show everyone that it's empty. Replace the Large Box over the Medium Box. Then pick up the Medium Box and show that it's empty too. Your friends will see through the diamond shape and think that they are looking inside the empty Large Box. **Actually, they are seeing the velvet-covered side of the Small Box.** Replace the Medium Box inside the Large Box, say a magic word and then reach inside and take out the orange from the Small Box.

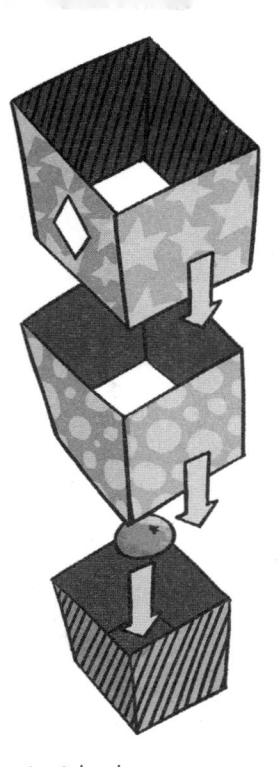

The Medium and Large Boxes can be decorated in many ways and the illusion can be used to tell lots of stories. For example, you could cover the boxes in **mysterious symbols** and say that they belonged to a great wizard, or maybe you could make them look like some scientific apparatus and explain that they allow you to move objects through time and space. Perhaps you can make them look like gift boxes and produce a birthday present for your friend. Could you make the trick out of tubes rather than boxes?

Or use one box and one tube? **How could you decorate the boxes and tubes, and what story could you tell?**

Once you are comfortable with the tricks in this book, you can get super creative and combine and change them. For instance, you could have several cards with a different type of fruit drawn on each one. Your friend chooses one of the cards and their selected fruit appears in the box! That would combine the P.A.T.E.O. Force from the section 'Superpower 7: Improve Focus and Boost Your Brain Power' with The Magic Boxes. How about asking someone to choose a playing card and saying that your notebook contains that card. You then flick through the notebook and show that every page contains drawings of different playing cards. Then you explain that you are joking, blow on the book and show that every page contains a drawing of their chosen card. That would combine Criss-Cross with The Book of Magic. **How could you combine and change the tricks?**

DARE TO BE DIFFERENT

Over the years, many magicians have created new and original ways of presenting magic.

Adelaide Herrmann was born in 1853 and at the time it was unusual for women to perform magic on stage. However, Adelaide really wanted to star in her own magic show. She worked hard and developed an original show in which she wore beautiful costumes and performed remarkable feats, including levitating high above the stage and even being fired from a cannon! She became famous as the **Queen of Magic**, and **encouraged other women to be creative and to pursue their dreams**.

The late Argentinian magician René Lavand lost his right hand in a car accident when he was nine years old. Fascinated by magic, he was forced to **create new ways of carrying out secret actions and performing tricks**. His presentations and shows had a wonderful, original, poetic and artistic quality to them. In one trick, Lavand shows three small balls and a teacup. He slowly places two of the balls into the cup and the third into his pocket. The ball from Lavand's pocket then magically appears in the cup. The master magician repeats the trick again and again, as he recites a beautiful Chinese poem written thousands of years ago. Lavand became famous and toured the world, presenting his original and inspirational magic.

One of my friends is Piff the Magic Dragon: on stage he looks like a big green dragon and his act is very funny. He started performing in small theatres and everyone loved what he was doing because it was so different and exciting. He worked hard and now has his own show in Las Vegas. Piff **dared to be different** and has become very successful.

Magic gives you an opportunity to make new and interesting props, and to create fun and interesting presentations. This sort of **creativity is also important in everyday life**. At the moment, the population of the Earth is around eight billion people. That's a huge number. However, there is **no one else out there who is like you**.

No one else smiles exactly like you, or feels exactly like you, or uses their imagination exactly like you. Use your creativity to celebrate who you are and how you think. Play and have fun. Make something new out of what you have around you. **Tell your story and change the world.**

REMEMBER THAT THERE IS NO ONE IN THE WHOLE WORLD WHO IS JUST LIKE YOU. USE THE POWER OF YOUR CREATIVITY TO IMAGINE WHAT MIGHT BE AND TELL STORIES THAT ARE MAGICAL AND UNIQUE.

FINALE

We are reaching the end of our time together. At the start, I said that there would be lots of surprises along the way. There has been one threaded through the entire book. Here are the eight chapters . . .

Increase your confidence by magic

Achieve the impossible with some incredible illusions

Make friendships appear

Master magical teamwork

Ace resilience

Grow your curiosity

Improve focus and boost your brainpower

Conjure up creativity

Do you notice anything odd? If you haven't spotted it yet, look at the first letter of each title. That's right, they spell out . . .

I AM MAGIC

And you are. At the start of the book, you might have wondered whether you could become a magician. Now you can do **lots of amazing things**, like **make a sausage float before your eyes, predict the future, produce an orange from an empty box, manipulate playing cards, become a human calculator, read your friend's mind and much more**.

In addition, you have discovered how **the power of magic** helps you to **boost your confidence, solve problems, make more friends, be a great team player, cope when things don't go to plan, cultivate your curiosity, focus your attention and be super creative**. These eight skills are important in everyday life, and together they will help you to grow and to change. And that is the real magic of magic.

So, have a great life and . . .

Arrgghhh! Hold on . . . I forgot something! There is one last surprise. At the start of the book, I promised to show you my favourite trick . . .

HOW TO CHANGE A TEA TOWEL INTO A CHICKEN!

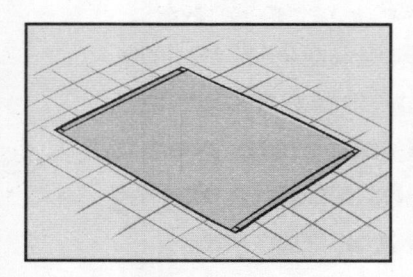

Here we go. For this final illusion you need a tea towel.

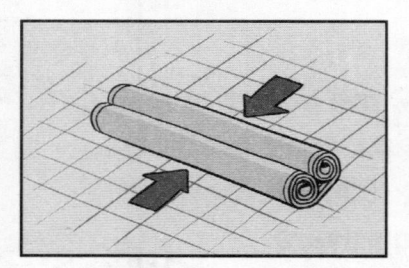

Lay the tea towel on a table and roll up each of the longer sides until they meet in the centre. This creates two tubes.

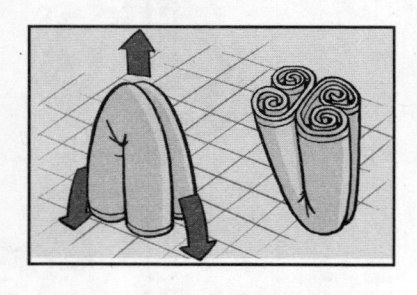

Next, fold the tea towel in half so that the ends of the two tubes touch.

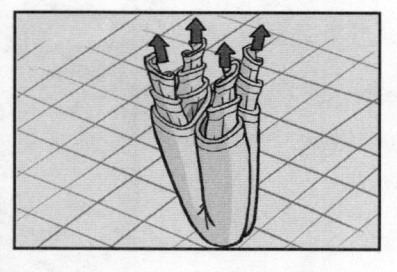

Then pull out each of the four corners, and grasp two of the corners in one hand and the other two in the other hand.

Pull hard and suddenly you have a chicken! Well, kinda. It's a fun stunt that I have performed for over twenty years! It always puts a smile on people's faces, and I hope that you can use it to make your friends and family happy.

Thank you so much for joining me on our journey into the strange and fascinating world of illusion. I hope that you had a good time. Now put this book down, get out there and enjoy your magical life!

Your Magical Journey

When I started out in magic I kept a notebook. Maybe you can do the same!

Here is a list of all the tricks, techniques and superpowers in the book. You could copy the list into your notebook and tick off each trick as you learn the secret and master the illusion!

You could also use the notebook to record your progress by writing down the first few times that you showed someone a certain trick, how everything went and how you can improve your performance in the future.

In another section you could make a note of the magicians that you see perform. What did you like and dislike about their performance? What did you learn from them?

Finally, your notebook is also a great place to jot down any ideas that you have for new tricks or interesting ways of presenting your magic, along with information that you discover about magic clubs, magazines and books.

Over time, your notebook will become a fascinating record of your magical journey.

Superpower 1: Increase Your Confidence
- THE FLOATING SAUSAGE!
- MIND CONTROL!
- THE BENDY PENCIL
- THE AMAZING JUMPING BAND

Superpower 2: Achieve the Impossible
- THE TIE-A-KNOT PUZZLE
- HOW TO PUT YOUR HEAD THROUGH A POSTCARD
- THE PREDICTION

Superpower 3: Make Friendships Appear
- THE MYSTERIOUS NAPKIN
- THE ZOMBIE'S FINGER
- WHAT'S THAT BEHIND YOUR EAR?
- THE FLOATING CUP
- YOU ARE ACE!

Superpower 4: Master Teamwork
- FIVE IN A ROW
- THE VANISHING COIN
- THE MIND READER

Superpower 5: Ace Resilience
- IS THIS YOUR CARD?
- THE PERAMBULATING PAPERCLIP

Superpower 6: Grow Your Curiosity
- THE SENSATIONAL STRAW
- MATTER THROUGH MATTER
- THINK OF A NUMBER
- THE MAGIC CIRCLES
- THE HUMAN CALCULATOR

Superpower 7: Improve Focus
- HAND TO HAND
- THE RIBBON SPREAD
- THE TWISTER
- SPELL-O-MATIC
- THE CHOICE IS YOURS

Superpower 8: Conjure up Creativity
- CRISS-CROSS CARD MAGIC
- THE BAFFLING BOOMERANGS
- THE BOOK OF MAGIC
- THE MAGIC BOXES

Finale
- HOW TO CHANGE A TEA TOWEL INTO A CHICKEN!

About the Author

Professor Richard Wiseman is a psychologist, author and magician. He has written several bestselling self-development books, created illusion-based YouTube videos that have attracted over 500 million views and carried out research into the relationship between magic and wellbeing. Richard recently received the prestigious Golden Grolla award for his work on psychology and magic. He has been described by Elizabeth Loftus (past president, Association for Psychological Science) as 'one of the world's most creative psychologists'.

Acknowledgements

Special thanks to David Britland and Will Houston for their expert guidance and comments. Thanks also to my friends and colleagues for allowing me to mention their amazing work. I would like to thank Jeff Wiseman, Jenny Hambleton and Caroline Watt for their invaluable help, along with my wonderful editors Anna Martin and Emily Lunn, the incredibly talented Luke Newell, and my magical agent Patrick Walsh.